THE EASTER SUNDAY
MASSACRE

A PROSECUTOR'S DIARY:
The True Story of
Mass Murderer James Ruppert

Karen Holcomb and John F. Holcomb

The Easter Sunday Massacre
A Prosecutor's Diary: The True Story of Mass Murderer James Ruppert

ISBN: 979-8-9885817-2-7

For information, contact the author:

Karen Holcomb
jkholcomb@twc.com

Published by:

Chilidog Press LLC
pbronson@chilidogpress.com

Chilidog Press
Milford, Ohio
www.chilidogpress.com

Cover design, interior design and typesetting:
Craig Ramsdell, RamsdellDesign.com

Dedication

For John M, Julie and Jack.

Contents

Introduction

I met John F. Holcomb in the 1990s, while I was working as the police and courts reporter for the *Hamilton Journal-News*. John, already a local legend, loomed larger than life. He possessed a booming voice, an air of gravitas, a razor-sharp wit and a deadpan delivery. During any trial, he commanded the courtroom, and you could hear a pin drop when he delivered an opening statement or closing argument. He was the only source I ever called "Sir." He was also the most quotable one I'd ever met. He referred to the electric chair as "Big Sparky" and coined the term "Lollipop Defense" ("The defendant says he committed this crime because his mommy didn't give him enough lollipops when he was growing up.").

Fast forward to 1996, when John became my father-in-law. (That's a whole other story.) One day he handed me a typed manuscript—a two-inch stack of 14-by-9-inch paper tucked into a brown accordion folder. It was the journal he had recorded throughout the James Ruppert investigation and trial. He had dictated daily updates into his Dictaphone and later had an assistant type it, knowing it would be the biggest case of his life. He asked me to turn this memoir into a book. I read the manuscript and considered it a powerful piece of storytelling. It reminded me of the Mickey Spillane mysteries John enjoyed reading, but this wasn't fiction. I tucked the manuscript into a drawer, fully planning to use it as the basis of a true-crime book. Then life became very busy. John's manuscript sat in that drawer for 24 years—until the pandemic.

In March 2020, most of the world closed down after COVID-19 spread around the globe. The school that employed me as a literacy tutor shut its doors until further notice, so I hunkered down with my family, venturing out only to buy groceries or refuel my car. During the first week or two, I had scrubbed my house clean and stenciled my laundry room floor in a gray and white Arabesque pattern, a la Pinterest. I was looking for a new project. Then I remembered John's manuscript. I took it from its drawer and began typing it into my computer, whittling it down while preserving John's unique personality and expletive-sprin-kled voice. As I finished the first day's work on the text, I glanced at the calendar on my desk. It was March 30, the day James Ruppert had gunned down 11 members of his family, 45 years earlier. That's when I knew I was meant to bring this book to fruition.

Because John's story needed some context, I added my own research. I read the multitude of media accounts about the Ruppert case and talked to people who were impacted by the tragedy. I conducted my socially distanced interviews on front porches, in open-air picnic shelters and, once, on the veranda of a nursing home. As a middle-school student when the mass murder occurred, I remembered how profoundly it affected my hometown back then. Four decades later, it still continued to do so.

A trigger warning: attitudes about women, mental illness, homo-sexuals, and even drinking and driving were quite different in 1975 than they are today. This book is not meant to glorify these perspectives, but to accurately capture a moment in time. These pages chronicle the inside story of the Ruppert case, the tragedy's collateral damage, and the chaos that ensued when a conservative small Midwestern town was faced with an overwhelming act of evil.

Sadly, John passed away in July 2000, and most of the other prin-cipals in the case have left us as well. But as the 50th anniversary of the Ruppert mass murder nears, the story's themes of good versus evil, the meaning of insanity, the role of religion, the power of greed and sibling rivalry remain as relevant as ever.

Chapter 1

The bells of St. Ann Catholic Church tolled three times a day, echoing over the streets of Lindenwald and muffling the rumbling and clacking of passing trains. A middle-class, predominately Catholic neighborhood on the southeast side of Hamilton, Ohio, Lindenwald stretched between the Great Miami River on the west and Dixie Highway on the east. Germans who settled the area named it for a grove of linden trees that grew on an early homestead. Lindenwald comprised a diverse mix of corner pubs, mom-and-pop shops, gritty manufacturing mills, parks, a bowling alley, a movie theater, and tidy Cape Cods, Craftsman bungalows, brick ranches, and tiny shotgun-style houses, like the one where Charity Ruppert lived. Lindenwald was a place where neighbors looked out for one another.

Charity, an elderly widow who attended Mass at St. Ann's every day, lived a short block from the parish, easily within walking distance. The "Angelus" bells so familiar to Charity—and all who resided in Lindenwald—sounded promptly at 6 a.m., noon and 6 p.m. Their purpose: to commemorate the Angel Gabriel's appearance to the Virgin Mary. Nine quick strokes, followed by a pause, then repeated three times, reminded the faithful to reflect on the Annunciation and recite three "Hail Mary" prayers with short verses in between.

On Easter Sunday 1975, Charity and her fellow St. Ann parishioners celebrated Mass on the holiest feast day of the Catholic calendar. Later that afternoon, Charity's son Leonard, his wife, Alma, and their eight children, ages 4 to 17, gathered at the Lindenwald residence for a family dinner. Charity's younger son, bachelor James Urban Ruppert, also lived at her house on 635 Minor Avenue. James, a skilled marksman and unemployed draftsman, slept late that Sunday. He had just turned 41 the day before, and had stayed out until the wee hours drinking beer at his favorite bar, The 19th Hole.

After genial conversation and an Easter egg hunt for the kids, Charity prepared a skillet of sloppy joes. The entree reflected her simple life-style and limited budget. As the Ruppert family gathered for the meal, the usual evening pealing of the Angelus called most Catholics in the community to meditate. But for all except one person in the house at 635 Minor Avenue, it served as their death knell.

James padded down the stairs with three loaded handguns and a rifle, and let loose a barrage of gunfire on his unsuspecting family. When the shooting ceased, 11 lifeless bodies sprawled across the kitchen and living room. Blood seeped through the floorboards. And James Ruppert stretched out on the couch to contemplate his swath of destruction.

Chapter 2

Hamilton Police Officers Terry Roberts and Sam Hopkins were patrolling in the two-man "bowl car" that chilly Easter night—March 30, 1975—in the area known as the city's Second Ward neighborhood. Though the bowl car made the rounds through the town's highest-crime area, it was a quiet night on the beat. Wind gusts, intermittent snow showers, and a wind-chill factor that dipped into the single digits kept most people indoors. Around 9:30 p.m., dispatch notified the bowl car that a call had just been received.

"A man has been shot," a male voice tersely reported by phone to the dispatcher.

The caller included no details other than the location of the shooting: 635 Minor Avenue.

Roberts and Hopkins headed that way. Roberts had been on the force for two years—long enough to know that such calls typically amounted to very little. "Most of the time, the problem has calmed down when you get there," Roberts said later. "We were not prepared for anything like what we saw that night."

Officer Bob Minor, who was on patrol only a few blocks from Charity's home, arrived first on the scene. Roberts and Hopkins pulled up behind him.

A short, clean-cut, dark-haired man with a slight build and a deeply dimpled chin stood in the front doorway of the house. He identified himself as James Ruppert. As Officer Minor approached the home, he glimpsed several bodies sprawled on the living room floor. Minor asked Ruppert how long he had been at the house. Ruppert answered that he'd been there since about five o'clock. He appeared "very calm" and spoke with an "unbroken" voice, Minor would testify at trial.

"Ruppert told us somebody had been shot inside," Roberts said. "Bob (Minor) didn't go too much further. I said, 'Bob, we should go in. There might be somebody alive that needs us.'"

Ruppert shook his head, signifying there were no survivors.

"Ruppert said something like, 'No. Nobody's alive,'" Roberts remembered.

Roberts walked through the front door into the small living room.

"There was brain matter all over," he said. "The first thing that came to my mind was hide and seek. There were people all over the floor and two or three guns on the table. I had never seen anything like that before. I had seen death a few times, but not kids. And I haven't seen anything that bad again."

Roberts saw the skillet of ground beef in the kitchen, and thought the killer had eaten a meal amidst the carnage. When he went back outside, he asked Ruppert if they should look for any other perpetrators involved in the crime. Ruppert said no.

Ruppert calmly asked if he could go back into the house to get his coat, as the temperature hovered around the zero mark, but the officers would not allow him to re-enter the crime scene. Roberts and Hopkins took him to police headquarters. "He was just as calm as he could be," Roberts said.

A crowd began to gather outside. As word spread that police were at the Ruppert house, the crowd grew.

Initially, Roberts said, the situation seemed surreal. Much later, as reality settled in, visceral images of that night would flash through his mind at inopportune moments.

"I can see the kids," he said. "And I was assuming they were trying to get away."

One child was near the front door, and another was near the back door.

"I never dream about it," Roberts added. "Sometimes, I can taste it. I'll be eating dinner, and I'll say, 'I don't want this steak anymore.' I can almost taste it, and it ruins my meal."

After completing his long shift, Roberts drove home and found his front door standing wide open. Chills went up his spine. His wife was out of town, and his nerves were raw from what he had witnessed on

Minor Avenue. He drew his gun and searched his house from top to bottom. No one was inside.

"I guess I didn't close the door all the way, and the wind blew it," he speculated.

It was a fitting end to a night he would never forget.

Chapter 3

JOHN HOLCOMB
Easter Sunday, March 30, 1975

I lingered in bed that morning, having stayed up until 1 or 1:30 a.m., coloring Easter eggs with my wife, Judy. I added some unusual touches to the eggs that year. I wrote "Pete Rose" on one, because my little 3-year-old, Jeffrey, loved the Cincinnati Reds second baseman known as "Charlie Hustle." For Mary Ann, my 7-year-old daughter, I wrote "Curly" on one (my nickname for her, which she disliked) and "Princess" on another. I remember putting "Big Shot John" on one for my oldest boy, John, who was 9, and "Jerk" on another one. I remember imagining that the kids would think what an unusual Easter rabbit it was that year. The rain from the previous Saturday night had changed to snow flurries, so I'd hidden the eggs around the first floor of my house.

At 11 a.m., I tuned in the *Hour of Power* church service conducted by Dr. Robert Schuller and televised from California. That Easter Sunday, the reverend preached his version of Jesus's Sermon on the Mount. My boy John joined me in bed, and we watched it together. As a matter of fact, I made my usual annual resolution to start going back to church again, since I hadn't been for many years. My wife took the kids frequently, but I hadn't been for a long time.

I had planned to shoot hoops on my backyard basketball court around noon, but the weather had turned too cold. Anyway, I had this big decision to make. Should I go in to work, as was my habit on Sunday afternoons, or stay home and watch the Cincinnati Reds play the Detroit Tigers in an exhibition game? I always worked every Sunday, because I accomplished exponentially more without the usual weekday distractions in the office. I could work from noon until 8:00 or 8:15 and make it home in time to watch my favorite TV detective series, *Kojak*. I decided to stay home and watch the Reds. The Reds took an early 8-0 lead, but I started to doze off about the sixth inning, when the Tigers tied it up. I figured the Reds would finish second in the West again that year.

I had my own private law practice, along with my elected position of Butler County Prosecuting Attorney. I made it to my office about 7:00 that night, got out my Dictaphone, and put a dent in the stack of work I'd sadly neglected from my private practice. Around 9 p.m., Assistant Prosecutor Dan Fischer sauntered in with a six-pack of Budweiser. He put it in the apartment-sized refrigerator I kept in the rear of my office, then he sat down and we shot the breeze for a while. After our chat, Dan went over to his office and started in on his own work.

At 10:10 p.m., my private line rang just as I was in the middle of dictating a deed. It was my good and dear friend, Glenn Ebbing, whom I loved like a brother. He was the finest homicide detective around, in my opinion. Not just in the city of Hamilton, but anywhere. He was tops. Because of my regard for him over the years in the many murder cases we'd worked together, we'd become close personal friends.

"Get down here right away, pal," came Glenn's familiar voice over the phone. "I've got eleven dead ones."

I thought it was another one of Glenn's gags.

"Huh?" I asked.

He repeated, "Get your ass down here, pal. I've got eleven dead bodies."

"What in the world is going on?" I asked.

"Goddammit, get your ass down here," Glenn said, and hung up the phone on me.

The first thing that went through my mind was some motorcycle gangs had a shootout. I walked over to Dan Fischer's office.

"Ebbing just called up and said he has eleven dead ones," I told him. "Do you want to go?"

As long as Dan had been in the Butler County Prosecutor's Office, I think he'd seen a dead body once, at the Grand Hotel, and that was the extent of his experience in the criminal division. He handled all the civil work.

"Well, yeah, I'll go," Dan replied.

Dan and I walked down the street to the Hamilton Police Department. Once inside, an officer directed us to a little side room. We knocked, walked in, and saw Ebbing (we called him "Jocko") sitting behind a desk.

Two uniformed officers—a couple of young patrolmen named Terry Roberts and Sam Hopkins—stood off in a corner.

Next to the desk sat a small, clean-cut-looking man dressed in a yellow long- sleeved shirt, white tie with a tie clasp, and plaid pants.

"Hi, Jimmy," Dan said to the man.

"Hi, Dan," the man said, standing up and shaking hands with Fischer, then sitting back down.

At that point, Ebbing spoke.

"We've got eleven dead members of the Ruppert family down at 635 Minor Avenue," he said.

I asked how this man seated beside the desk figured into it. Ebbing gave us the run-down. The man's name was James Urban Ruppert, a 41-year-old who had been laid off from his job as a drafts-man at Production Design in Dayton. He lived with his mother at 635 Minor Avenue. Ebbing had already read him his Miranda rights, and Ruppert indicated he wasn't going to waive his rights. He added that he didn't mind talking, as long as it wasn't related to the circumstances surrounding the shooting.

Ruppert told Ebbing he'd been home all day, had been wearing the same clothing since he got up at 3:00 that afternoon, and that his brother had arrived at the house around 4:00 with his large family. Ebbing asked him again if he had left the house at all that day, and Ruppert said not until the police arrived and drove him to the police station. When asked if he had any living relatives, Ruppert answered that he had only one: an aunt, Leona, in Wapakoneta, Ohio.

Detective Don "Red Dog" Gabbard then called from the crime scene to report that two guns lay in plain view on a living room table. When Ebbing asked Ruppert if the guns belonged to him, he affirmed that they did. Ruppert told Ebbing he had consumed no alcohol, illegal drugs, or prescription medication that day, but had "three or four beers yesterday." He denied using any drugs or taking any medication at all. This led Ebbing to ask if Ruppert had ever seen a psychiatrist. Ruppert replied that he had, but would not give the doctor's name until he had spoken to his lawyer about it.

Ebbing asked Ruppert the names of the people in the house. He named Mrs. Leonard (Charity) Ruppert, Leonard Ruppert Jr., Mrs. Alma Ruppert, Leonard Ruppert III, Carol Ruppert, Michael Ruppert, Tom Ruppert, and Dave Ruppert. He said there were three others, but he did not recall their names.

"That was the only thing that seemed to bother him," Officer Roberts recollected decades later. "That he couldn't remember all the names."

Ruppert balked when Ebbing asked him what happened in the residence.

"You can talk to my attorney about that," Ruppert answered. "I want a lawyer."

That was the point when Dan and I had walked into the room. Ruppert was leafing through a phone book.

"I see Bert Imfeld's name here," Ruppert said. "I went to school with him."

Ebbing dialed the number and handed Ruppert the phone. Once on the line, Imfeld obviously asked him what type of case it was, because I heard Ruppert say, "I'm a suspect in a homicide."

Ruppert hung up the phone.

"Imfeld doesn't take criminal cases, but he recommended Hugh Holbrock, so that's who I want," he said.

A recording at Holbrock's number directed callers to an alternate number, which belonged to his law partner, H.J. "Joe" Bressler. After phoning Bressler and telling him he was a suspect in a homicide,

Ruppert advised us that his attorneys would be at the station in about 20 minutes. Dan and I left with Detective Ron Wells, who drove us down to the house on Minor Avenue. It was around 10:30 p.m., and a police cruiser with flashing lights had one end of the street blocked.

"Boy, Police Chief McNally is really doing it up right again for the big PR," I thought.

After Wells dropped us off at the house, we saw about 500 spectators gathered on the opposite side of the street. Then I realized this wasn't just for PR. Chief McNally stood in front of the residence and told me I'd better go take a look. Over the last 11 years I'd been with the Butler County Prosecutor's Office, I'd seen some bad ones. I thought I'd seen everything. You name it, I'd seen it. Back in the summertime, after I'd seen Mrs. Doench[1] with that mattock buried in her face, I knew damn well I'd seen everything. But let me tell you, I was wrong. I was dead wrong. When I walked into that house, I saw a sight like I'd never seen. Five bodies lay in the living room, and six in the kitchen. The massive amount of blood from the victims dripped into the basement. But the thing that really stuck with me, and would haunt me for the rest of my life, was a little 4-year-old boy sprawled right next to the sofa, shot once in the side of the head, with vomit near his mouth. A chocolate Easter egg in a pink tinfoil wrapper lay just beyond his tiny fingers.

After I walked through the carnage, meticulously inspecting the scene, I left the house. The thing that gnawed at me was how

---

1 The gruesome nature of Mrs. Ruth Doench's murder caught the eye of national true-crime magazine *Front Page Detective*. In its June 1975 issue, the magazine profiled the February 9, 1975, slaying in the article "Madman With A Mattock." The victim, a 73-year-old former Hayes Elementary School principal who lived on Tylersville Road, just east of Hamilton, was cut above the right eye, on the right cheek, and on the forehead with a wood-cutting tool used by gardeners and landscapers. "Horribly, the mattock had been left there, the blade imbedded deeply into the forehead," the magazine reported. "If the woman had been alive when the mattock crashed into her head, blood would have spurted about the room, propelled by the force of pumping heart. But there was little blood. Clearly, the stab wounds evident in the area of her heart had killed the woman even before the killer had turned his savage attack to her head." Police later arrested and charged Donald Korn, a burly, 29-year-old, 220-pound, six-foot welder who had rented Doench's guest house about a year earlier. Police said Korn terrorized several women on a crime spree that included murder, attempted murder, and rape.

physically unaffected I was by that bloodbath. Maybe seeing human slaughter, especially of that magnitude, caused me to chain-smoke, or drink too much, or things like that. I didn't know. But I did know it was an eerie feeling to think that a sensitive, decent, conscientious man like myself could walk through a grisly scene like that without being physically sickened by it.

The very first murder I saw, on Christmas Eve 1964, bothered me. An old lady named Mrs. Strayer out on Vine Street had her throat slit. That one knocked me for a loop. I fought back the urge to vomit. From that point on, I gradually overcame that feeling. People often asked what effect these grisly murder scenes had on me. I always told them my first reaction was to fight the urge to get physically ill, because of the gory, bloody, messy violence of the thing. Lots of times they stank. My second reaction always was sadness, because a living human being, somebody's loved one, was dead and gone. My third reaction—and maybe the only one I still got, having evolved to this point over 11 years in this business—was to get damn mad. Not to sound like society's vindicator, or anything like that, but I got damn mad and carried it with me. I made up my mind to be hardnosed and bust my tail and make damn sure the defendant got everything he or she had coming under the law. That's the way I looked at this case.

Dan, on the other hand, had never seen anything like this. He looked like he was about to get sick. It really shook him up. We climbed into a cruiser with Patrolman Steve McDulin, who drove us back to the police station. By that time, Ebbing had bagged Ruppert's clothing, including his blood-spattered brown shoes, and tagged the items for analysis by the Bureau of Criminal Identification and Investigation lab in London, Ohio. BCI Agent Thorold Todd was already there. He took paraffin casts of Ruppert's hands to check for the presence of nitrates from unburned gunpowder. He scraped Ruppert's fingernails for traces of blood or other evidence. I noticed Ruppert's hands seemed very, very clean, but he had yellowish cigarette stains between the first two fingers of his left hand.

Ruppert, having changed to jail garb and sandals, went into another room to consult with attorneys Holbrock and Bressler in private. About an hour later, attorney Holbrock emerged from the room and asked us to go through Ruppert's wallet. We found a stack of notebook paper with various figures and notations from the stock market handwritten on the pages, a yellow title and registration slip to Ruppert's Volkswagen Beetle, a hundred-dollar bill, fifty-dollar bill, three singles, and 33 cents in change. Then Holbrock continued his consultation with Ruppert, and Ebbing and I went downstairs to the detective room.

The main thing that worried me, I told Ebbing, was we had 11 people dead down there on Minor Avenue, and if this Ruppert was some kind of a goddamned killer, I didn't want him out on the street while we fooled around trying to decide to charge him or not.

"Just tell me what we have here," I said to Ebbing.

"Well, the guy said he was home all day, and if he was home all day, he'd sure as hell have to know what happened," Ebbing said. "And he won't talk about what happened. And he said those guns were his."

It seemed pretty obvious that Ruppert's guns on the living room table were the murder weapons. That was something. But the clincher, for me, was the pair of brown shoes Ruppert wore. Ebbing pointed out that the blood spatter on the side could be the result of Ruppert walking through the crime scene. But the blood spray on the tops of the shoes, on the other hand, looked as if they came from a downward angle, indicating Ruppert was the shooter. I told Ebbing to go ahead and charge Ruppert with 11 counts of aggravated murder.

Chapter 4

Dan Fischer and James Ruppert had both graduated from Hamilton Catholic High School. A year separated them, so they were acquainted, but not close friends. Ruppert had no close friends in high school and was known as a loner. The student body numbered only about 200, so all the boys knew each other by name. Fischer also knew Leonard Ruppert, James's older brother. Everyone called Leonard "Pinky" because he had "fiery red hair," Fischer recalled.

In the years after graduation, Fischer often saw James Ruppert at the local stock brokerage.

"I was really impressed," the attorney said. "I thought that he had become really wealthy. I was mistaken. He hadn't."

Like Holcomb, Fischer had a private law practice, along with his job at the Butler County Prosecutor's Office.

"In those days I went back to the office every night," he said.

March 30, 1975, held significance to Fischer for several reasons: It was his wife's birthday, it was Easter Sunday, and it was the night he saw the most horrific sight of his life. It would stick with him for the rest of his days.

"All of a sudden, John came walking to my office real fast, and he was real flustered," Fischer recalled. "He told me about the phone call he'd gotten, and he asked, 'You want to get in on this?'"

He did, indeed. When the two men arrived at the police station in the Hamilton Municipal Building, Fischer immediately recognized his former schoolmate James Ruppert sitting with a detective.

"I said, 'Hi, Rupe,' and shook hands with him," he said.

Fischer sensed something different about Ruppert and backed away.

"He seemed to be kind of defensive," he said. "I just got as far away from him as I could after that. I never spoke to him again."

When they arrived at the crime scene on Minor Avenue later that night, Chief McNally and Coroner Garrett Boone were outside, along with hundreds of spectators behind crime tape.

"The word got around so fast," Fischer said. "We still didn't know who'd done it, and I felt uneasy standing there. We went inside—and I'm not exaggerating now—we were literally stepping over the bodies of all the children."

Little John Ruppert, only 4 years old and the youngest of them all, was curled into the fetal position. The sight disturbed Fischer so much, the first thing he did when he returned to his office was head straight to the refrigerator and grab a cold beer. He remembered being interviewed by television reporters for an hour or two, then getting home around 4 a.m.

"It was so hard to get to sleep, seeing all these children with bullet holes in them," Fischer said. "I wanted to try to forget about it, but I couldn't. I couldn't get that out of my mind."

Instead of forgetting the horrific crime scene, Fischer would end up delving much deeper into the case. Although he specialized in civil work, he would become one of the three men sitting at the prosecution table during Ruppert's murder trial.

Chapter 5

Jᴏʜɴ Hᴏʟᴄᴏᴍʙ
Monday, March 31, 1975

When Dan and I returned to the office, it was around 2 a.m.

"How about a cold one?" he asked.

I remembered the six-pack of Bud that Dan had put in my icebox earlier that night.

"Yeah, that sounds pretty good right now," I said.

Someone banged on the door as Dan rattled around in the refrigerator. There stood Tom Adkins, an impressive, personable guy with Channel 5 News, accompanied by two cameramen. I swear to God, I was so embarrassed, because Adkins was dressed like a million bucks, sharper than hell, with his shoes shined and a nice pair of slacks, and a long leather jacket with a turtleneck sweater underneath. And here stood old John, wearing dirty buck shoes, a pair of old green-and-gray plaid denim slacks—which were so worn they had a hole in the hip pocket—and a short-sleeved sport short. I could see myself all over television in Southwestern Ohio, looking like a damn rube, with people asking, "Who's that damn rube prosecutor up in Hamilton?"

I put on my red, waist-length windbreaker jacket to cover my sloppy attire and did a brief interview about the murders.

"Boy, I sure could use a beer," one of the cameramen said after we'd wrapped. "You guys got anything?"

When Dan went back for a beer for the guy, I'd like to have died. Hell, you get so you distrust the press sometimes, because of some of the tricks they pull. But Fischer gave all three of them a cold one, along with reporter Dick Perry from the *Cincinnati Post*. Perry had walked back from the police station with us. We all drank our beers together.

As soon as that crew departed, Channel 9 showed up, then Channel 12, and then the *Associated Press*. I got exasperated when the *Associated Press* guy started asking about the death penalty. It was too early for that call. Hell, I was sure we had arrested the right man, but I wasn't sure we had enough evidence yet. I was pinning my hopes on the crime lab turning up more proof.

By the time Dan and I left the office, it was 4:30 a.m. I was wide-awake and keyed-up, so I went down to my basement at home and got myself a Hudepohl beer. When I finally went upstairs and climbed into bed, all I could visualize was that 4-year-old little boy on that floor. I didn't know if it was because I had a son, Jeff, roughly the same age, but I kept picturing that little tyke there, the expression on his face, the way his body lay sideways on the floor, the tennis shoes he had on.

Then I got out of bed, knelt at the side of it, and said the Lord's Prayer. It had been so long since I'd said it, I wasn't even sure I had the words right. I asked God to bless my wife and my children and those poor little kids in that house on Minor Avenue. I went back to bed and lay there awake, thinking about that 4-year-old boy for another half an hour. Just as I'd finally drifted off, the damn phone rang. It was Ebbing calling at 5:30 a.m.

"The chief wants to know if you think it's a good idea to put Patrolman Barnickle in a cell with Ruppert," Ebbing said. "You know, put him in there dressed like a prisoner, put some dirt on his face, some rags on him, and throw him in there like he's coming off a drunk or something. Maybe get Ruppert to talk to him a little bit."

"Yeah, I think that's a good idea," I answered. "You didn't have to call me up to ask me that."

"OK, Pal," Ebbing said.

He laughed because he knew he'd annoyed me by waking me up, then he hung up the phone.

I got about another hour's sleep before the alarm sounded at 7:00. I didn't have time to shave. When I was in the bathroom showering, the phone started to ring. The first two were jerks from the Dayton papers. I understood newsmen had a job to do, but Dayton newsmen were jerks. Creeps. They badgered you, asked phony questions, reversed questions, and drew inferences from things you didn't even say. They were cheap-shot artists, and besides that, they were the ones who always called at 7:00 in the morning.

Anyway, when I got to the office, the BCI agents were gathering evidence at Minor Avenue, and the autopsies were being performed on the 11 bodies (a task which would take three days). All I could do was sit tight until the evidence started trickling in.

Then the phone calls starting coming from all over hell. The *AP* from Washington, *Mutual Broadcasting* from Washington, The *New York Times*, a radio station in Cleveland, another in Columbus. I spent most of the day on the phone, and of course, the local reporters dropped in from time to time.

Despite all the media attention, the enormity of the crime had yet to sink in with me. The realization first hit when I saw the headline in Monday's *Middletown Journal*: "Local mass slaying said to be largest for one family."

Chapter 6

The murders stunned the entire city of Hamilton and beyond. The dead were Charity "Billie" Ruppert, 65; her son Leonard II, 42; his wife, Alma, 38; and their eight children: Leonard III, 17; Michael, 16; Thomas, 15; Carol, 13; Ann, 12; David, 10; Teresa, 9; and John, 4.

Leonard, an engineer for General Electric, resided one town over, in Fairfield, Ohio, with his large, close-knit family. They had attended Easter Vigil at Sacred Heart Church on Saturday evening, so they could spend Easter Sunday visiting relatives. Early in the day, the family had called on Alma's mother in New Burlington, Ohio. Then they arrived at Charity's home around 5 p.m. A neighbor had spotted Little John hunting for Easter eggs in the front yard shortly after their arrival.

"They were all such nice kids," family friend Lucille Tabler said.

Friends described Alma as "the epitome of a good neighbor," a devoted mother, an avid gardener, and a religious, somewhat shy woman. Her husband, Leonard, was a pillar of the community.

Neighbors characterized the suspect, James Ruppert, as "intelligent," an "ardent reader" and "a loner" with an interest in guns. The adjective used most frequently was "quiet."

Charity, who had lived in Lindenwald for more than 20 years, was considered a good neighbor and a religious, family-oriented woman.

Despite the close proximity of the small homes, neighbors reported hearing no gunshots or arguments at the Ruppert residence on the day of the murders. The first sign of trouble came when police arrived just after 9:30 p.m., and were greeted at the door by the 41-year-old Ruppert, who stood 5-feet, 5-inches tall. His .22-caliber semiautomatic rifle still leaned against the refrigerator and his three other handguns were placed around the living room. The only sign of a struggle inside was an overturned wastebasket. Several Easter baskets contained candy and colorful eggs, and a skillet of sloppy joes remained in the kitchen.

Police on the scene enlisted the help of Larry Fullerton—a photographer for the local newspaper, the *Hamilton Journal-News*—to photograph the victim's bodies. He took shots of the dead in the kitchen and prepared to walk back outside.

"Wait," he was told. "There are more in the living room."

Also stunned by the extensive carnage was John Janco, another *Journal-News* photographer, who waited outside. When the police wheeled out a stretcher with a white sheet covering the youngest child's body, the spectators gasped. Janco snapped a photo and prepared to head back to the newsroom to develop his film. But then, another stretcher followed closely behind. It stopped him in his tracks. When each subsequent sheet-draped body was wheeled out, the spectators groaned and Janco shot another picture. *Journal-News* reporter Jim Newton described it as a "parade of death" that "continued for more than 15 minutes." The last body taken from the home was Alma's. The Hamilton Police Department's fleet of six station wagons transported each victim to a local funeral home, then made a return trip for the other five.

Nick Dadabo, a deeply religious man and the first Eucharistic minister in the Archdiocese of Cincinnati,[2] distributed Communion to Leonard Ruppert's family the night before they died. A large crowd of worshippers—between 600 and 700—had attended Mass at Sacred Heart that evening. Afterward, Dadabo hurried to his father's pizza joint, Chester's Pizzeria, to help out with the rush.

"We were busy that night," he recalled.

Shortly after the mass, Leonard Ruppert walked in the pizzeria, with a couple of his children in tow, to pick up an order.

"He was a very nice, good family man," said Dadabo. "Respectful to his mom and wife and kids. Just really nice kids—all of them."

Ironically, Leonard's brother, suspect Jim Ruppert, also picked up a Chester's pizza about half an hour after his brother did. Jim Ruppert was a regular customer, and Dadabo still remembered his usual order:

---

2 The first non-ordained layman appointed to assist in the distribution of communion elements.

a 9-inch sausage pizza he carried out and took to his favorite bar, the 19th Hole, in the Hamilton Plaza.

"He would come in, get his pizza," Dadabo said, four decades after the murders. "He didn't say very much. He was strange. I remember his mother saying, 'I wish Jimmy would find somebody.'

"I go from knowing this family, to giving Leonard and his family the last Eucharist they got, and one hour later getting them a pizza," he said.

The next day, which was Easter Sunday, Dadabo heard multiple sirens and followed the sound to Minor Avenue to see what was amiss. A crowd already had gathered in the street, as word traveled that some sort of tragedy had occurred in the usually peaceful neighborhood. Dadabo saw Office Minor vomiting in the front yard next to a hand-cuffed James Ruppert.

Because he was a parish council member and knew the Ruppert family well, Dadabo helped plan the funeral at Sacred Heart.

"The outpouring of grief, respect, community and love that was shown there was very emotional," he said. "The priests had tears coming down. It was such a nice family. This is what makes it so hard. Their souls had to go right to heaven. People need to know the horror of it, but they also need to know this was a wonderful Catholic, Christian family. They surely are sitting at the right hand of God."

Chapter 7

John Holcomb
Monday, March 31, 1975

I tried to nap right after supper, as was my usual custom. My wife, Judy, always tried to get me to call it "dinner," but my Mom and Dad called it "supper," so I called it "supper." Judy was a doctor's daughter and was what you might call well-bred. She was genteel, not stuck-up or snotty. Don't get the wrong idea. But those were the kinds of people she had as friends. On the other hand, she often told me—and I know it's true—that I didn't like anybody unless he was an electrician, a plumber, a carpenter or a policeman. Anyway, after supper I wasn't able to nap. My little kids gathered around the television, anxious to see the old man on the evening news. I was on one of the stations; maybe it was Channel 5 with Tom Adkins.

"Oh, Daddy looks like Kojak," Mary Ann, my 7-year-old, commented, referring to the bald detective in my favorite TV show.

I was still taking phone calls from all over hell, but fortunately, nobody called during the Kentucky-UCLA championship game that evening. I really thought Kentucky had the better team, even though they didn't pull off the win. I thought Kevin Grevey—the local boy who was attorney Norm Grevey's kid—outshone every other player on the basketball court with his game high of 34 points. I was just so proud of him. During the game, one of the announcers mentioned the Ruppert murders, because they had taken place in Grevey's hometown.

After the game, I drove over to my dad's house on the West Side of Hamilton with two cans of Hudepohl beer. I wanted to talk to him, because he was the smartest guy I'd ever known. He taught school all of his life. He hailed from the hills of Kentucky,

21

and attended Miami University during the day while working the night trick at Armco Steel. He earned his master's degree and was just a few hours shy of his PhD. That was only because he couldn't get the residency he needed, having a wife and five kids he couldn't afford to leave. He painted houses in the summertime instead. He'd have been a fine doctor or lawyer. He could have been anything.

Anyway, I felt the need to talk to him about this feeling that haunted me, this feeling that I could walk into the carnage on Minor Avenue and not be physically affected by it like Dan Fischer was. As we sipped our beer, he advised me it was nothing to be worried about; it just meant I was a professional at my job. He compared it to a doctor who deals with terminal illness on a daily basis and doesn't get upset. Under different circumstances, it would tear me apart, he told me. But in my line of work, I had become accustomed to murder scenes and thought of them in terms of a job.

Then we talked about a newborn calf on the farm we owned outside of town and a few other things like that. When he realized I felt better, he announced it was time for him to go to bed. I slept pretty well that night, but I still could not get the picture of little 4-year-old John Ruppert out of my mind. Something inside me knew I was going to see that image as long as I lived.

Chapter 8

Two unanswered questions remained in the "puzzling aftermath" of the Easter slaying, according to the *Hamilton Journal-News* April 1, 1975, edition. Police said 44 gunshots had been fired, but why didn't neighbors hear anything? And why weren't any of the 11 Rupperts able to escape the house on Minor Avenue before they were all gunned down?

The small residence had only a living room in front and a kitchen directly behind it, with a small bathroom off to the side. The back door in the kitchen could be seen from the front door in the living room, the hallmark of a so-called shotgun house. One of the victims, 13-year-old Carol, lay just inside the back door in a pool of blood. The house next door was only a few feet away.

A different matter altogether puzzled Arthur H. Bauer, a friend of James Ruppert.

"He's not violent at all," Bauer told the *Journal-News*. "I can't believe he did it. I'd sure like to talk to him... He never got mad. That's what disturbs me."

Like the others who knew Ruppert, Bauer described him as a quiet man who spent many hours at the Lane Public Library in downtown Hamilton and at the local Hayden-Stone stock brokerage. Ruppert lived with his mother off and on over the years, but Bauer recalled the suspect had resided in an apartment when he worked days and attended night school at the University of Cincinnati. Ruppert eventually quit school and took a job with an engineering firm in Cincinnati. The job required him to travel, which worried his mother.

As James Ruppert's acquaintances puzzled over his arrest, friends and relatives of the innocent victims remembered them as the All-American family. Leonard, the breadwinner; Alma, the stay-at-home mom; and their eight children who attended Catholic schools (except for John, who was too young). Their comfortable two-story home on Walter Avenue in Fairfield was five doors away from attorney Jim Irwin's.

"That was the best-looking, smartest bunch of kids I've ever seen," Irwin said.

During the school year, Irwin drove Lenny and Mike Ruppert, who were sophomores, to Badin High School with his own son, Greg, who was also a sophomore. Mike and Greg were best friends. Although he was just a teen, Mike had made quite an impression on the Irwin family. Mike knew the names of all the plants in the Irwin's greenhouse, and even brought them a cocoon to keep inside the space.

"Keep it in here," he'd told them. "It will open into a beautiful butterfly."

Just before he died, Mike had painted a picture of a potted flower with the words "Keep On Growin'?"as an Easter gift for Greg. Greg hung it on his bedroom wall.

Another Ruppert brother, Tommy, had inherited his father's mechanical ability. He easily leveled all the plant tables in the Irwins' greenhouse.

Littlest brother John was remembered as a ray of light.

"John was always smiling," said Jim Irwin's wife, Pat. "He had the sunshiniest smile!"

When Alma was a young woman, she loved going to dances, restaurants and movies with both Leonard and Jim Ruppert. Alma's mother, Edna Allgeier, told the local newspapers that Alma would always sit between the two brothers in the front seat of their truck. When Leonard tired of being a threesome and asked Alma to choose one brother as her boyfriend, she chose Leonard. Jim never got over it, according to Allgeier.

Allgeier had liked Jim, and even thought he'd make a good boyfriend for one of her other daughters. She had long been friends with his mother, Charity, and had never heard her say an unkind word about Jim.

Jim and Leonard were close, and Leonard acted as a surrogate father to his younger brother after their dad passed away when the boys were adolescents. Jim served as best man at Alma and Leonard's wedding. The newlyweds, who were avid square-dancers, performed for their guests at their own reception. They continued to participate in square dances throughout their marriage.

Rufus "Bud" Skinner, of Kissimmee, Florida, recalled how family vacations were important to his nephew Leonard. Leonard packed his entire family into his van and drove them to Uncle Bud's house one summer. The proud uncle described Leonard, a former Navy man with a lifelong interest in electronics, as a successful engineer who had recently traveled to Brazil for an extended work project. When he wasn't working, Leonard was a family man who loved to participate in Boy Scout activities with his sons.

Alma also donated her time to the community. She volunteered in the Sacred Heart church office, collected for Easter seals, and helped Mike with his paper route. She loved taking neighbor kids on outings with her own, and packed peanut butter and jelly sandwiches for the trips. She baked cookies that she shared with her neighbors, loved to garden and longed to live on a farm.

At Sacred Heart School, where five of the young Rupperts were enrolled, the Rev. John Roettele—who was new to the parish—described the student body as "all broken up." The same was true at Badin High School, where students planned to show up *en masse* to the funeral.

On the evening of Thursday, April 3, 1975, more than 600 people gathered at Sacred Heart Church for the Ruppert family's Mass of Christian Burial. The pallbearers carried the white pall-draped caskets one by one, with little John again being the first. Seven Catholic priests officiated. Cincinnati's Archbishop, the Most Rev. Joseph Bernadin, sent a message of condolence to be read during the service. Bernardin had visited Alma's family right after the murders.

"Things happen to disturb and upset," Fr. Roettele told those assembled for the funeral Mass. "Events occur that are disgusting and revolting—some happen to shock and terrify us; some to depress and demoralize us. The darkness is all around us, but in the darkness, we, too, have to find the light that is Christ."

After the service, the Rupperts' bodies lay in state at the church overnight, with the 11 caskets arranged to form a cross. Early the next morning, a procession of 11 hearses carried the Rupperts to their final resting place at Arlington Memorial Gardens in Cincinnati. As the mourners followed the long line of hearses and said their final farewells, an 11-count indictment for aggravated murder was issued for Jim Ruppert, who remained in the Butler County Jail without bond. Ruppert declined to attend the funeral, choosing instead to remain alone in his cell.

Chapter 9

Greg Irwin served as a "double pallbearer" at the Ruppert family funeral. As Mike Ruppert's best friend and classmate at Stephen T. Badin Catholic High School, Irwin was charged with assembling a team of pallbearers from the student body. Six people typically carried a casket, and with a procession of 11 caskets, 66 pall-bearers were needed.

"Being Catholics, we didn't like that number," Greg said.

Instead, 48 Badin students were chosen. Each carried a coffin into church, then some returned to help carry a second one.

"There were 11 hearses," Greg said. "Every one in the county was used, and one had to be brought in from somewhere else."

The Mass of Christian Burial, and especially the music performed by Ed Goodfriend, "was incredible," Irwin remembered. It didn't make saying goodbye to his best friend any easier, though.

The two neighbors had become friends in junior high school and forged a close bond playing in Mike's backyard clubhouse, driving to school together every day, and riding their 10-speed Schwinn bicycles down their street.

"They used to ride their bikes awful good," Irwin said of the Ruppert brothers. "Lenny did wheelies all the way down the street."

Lenny was big and strong, and Mike was "kind of a nerd, but funny, and a real smart kid." His nickname was "Possum," maybe because he was quiet, but no one knew for sure. He could be a real goofball, too.

"One time he got mad at the gym teacher, and just ran home," Irwin recalled.

Another time, Mike left a bottle of Scope mouthwash on the desk of a teacher known for his bad breath.

Mike liked Greg's sister. He showed up at their house with gifts for both of them on the Good Friday before he died.

Greg and Mike had talked about having a secret sign, just the two of them, to go along with their clubhouse and to symbolize their friendship. Greg suggested the sign his dad always gave him when he went off to work: linking his two index fingers to form a chain, signifying solidarity.

"That's what it meant," Greg said. "We're solid."

As Mike left the Irwin house that Good Friday at twilight, Greg heard the phone ring and rushed inside to answer it. Mike pushed the door open for a split-second and flashed the new sign to his best buddy.

"Hey, Greg," he said, tugging his intertwined index fingers.

Greg reciprocated.

"That was the only time we ever used the sign," he said.

Two days later, Irwin heard the phone ring in the middle of the night.

"It was one or two in the morning," he said. "I heard my dad talking. I thought, 'Uh-oh, something very unusual is going on.' I just heard him say something about 'How many bodies?'"

They lived in a tri-level, and Greg yelled up to ask his dad what was happening.

His dad, he noticed, had been crying, but quickly tried to compose himself. He answered that everything was fine. When his dad returned to his upstairs bedroom, Greg heard him crying again. He climbed the stairs and begged his father to disclose what had happened.

"He said, 'The Rupperts were all murdered,'" Greg recalled. "I remember asking him—'*Even Mike?*'—and he said, 'Yes. They were all killed by their uncle.'"

Almost five decades after the murders, tears stream down Irwin's face when he discusses that night. "It always happens whenever I talk about this," he said. "That moment is etched in my mind forever."

His mind shut down for a while after the murders, perhaps a defense mechanism to protect his psyche from the shock, horror and grief, he speculates.

After a week of Easter break, students returned to Badin. There was no mention of the tragedy, no grief counselor on hand, no therapy dog. It was 1975, long before such measures were even considered.

"We all just went back to school on Monday," Irwin said. "You drive to school the next day, and they (the Ruppert children) are just not there."

During the afternoon announcements, a list of students who were supposed to stay after school for a meeting blared over the speaker. The last name announced was Mike Ruppert's.

"There was just silence for 10 or 15 seconds," Irwin said. "It was so surreal."

Chuck Mignery, another classmate of Mike and Lenny, remembered returning to school that Monday and seeing the two empty desks in his homeroom. The image tore him apart. On Easter Sunday, Chuck had been at his grandmother's home, only six houses away from the Minor Avenue murder scene. On the way home to Fairfield, his family drove past the house, not knowing that his friends' entire family lay dead inside. It was around 8:00 in the evening.

"There was no commotion, no police cars—nothing yet," Chuck said. "But when I went by there, they were all dead."

The next morning, his mother was watching the NBC morning news, and Chuck saw a photograph of the Ruppert family appear on the screen. Initially, he was excited to see his friends on the national news.

"I'll never forget it 'til the day I die," he said. "I said, 'Look, Mom, the Rupperts are on TV!"

His mom told him to just keep watching, so he did. Then he heard that the family had been murdered. Chuck rode his bike to Minor Avenue to see for himself what was happening at the house.

"It was cordoned off," he said. "You couldn't get near it."

Later that day, Chuck and a friend rode their bikes to a job they worked moving gravel during Easter break. On the way, they passed Leonard Ruppert's house. The family dog was still in the backyard.

"You could hear that dog barking," Chuck said. "It was an eerie sound."

Chapter 10

John Holcomb
Tuesday, April 1 to Sunday, April 6, 1975

Reports filtered in from the crime lab little by little.

BCI Agent Steve Molnar Jr., located 26 cartridge casings fired from one of the pistols—an Astra .22 nine-shot—found in the house. That meant Ruppert had loaded that gun three times during the massacre.

Another agent, Dave Nibert, identified two of Ruppert's left-hand fingerprints on the Astra—one on the barrel and one on the trigger guard.

I was still dealing with the usual onslaught of phone calls from the press. I returned to the office that night, after going home and changing my clothes, and continued to sort through reports and work on the case. I called my buddy Ebbing at home about 10:00, and his wife told me he was probably down at the Coachlite Bar.

"If he's at the Coachlite tonight, he's got good cause to be there, because he's been watching those autopsies for the last two days," I told her.

On my way home I stopped at the Coachlite. It wasn't what you'd call one of the finer establishments in town. I'd never been there before, but Glenn assured me it was OK, because a former neighbor of his owned the bar. I drank two or three beers with Glenn before we both went home. I slept pretty well that night, or at least, better.

By Wednesday, April 2, I didn't want to talk to any member of the press, be on TV, or have my picture taken. I just wanted to be left alone so I could do my damn job the best I could without being bothered with a bunch of stupid questions that didn't amount to anything. What good was it going to do the public to know what the autopsy report said? Why did they have to know how many times somebody was shot in the head or in the back? You get to a point when you want to refuse to cooperate with the press at all and just tell them "no comment" to everything. They get in a contest with each other; each one trying to outdo the other.

I went to the Fraternal Order of Police Lodge that night and had a meatloaf supper, which was passable. I went there on the first Wednesday of every month, because I was the FOP's legal adviser, and besides it was a place to go and let your hair down a little bit and relax with the policemen. It was all stag, all men. It was the one night a month I could relax with my friends. But those news hounds, if they could peg you at a certain place and time, they never forgot it. Really, they were better snoops than detectives in a lot of ways.

Around 8:00, I got a telephone call at the FOP Lodge from Dick Perry of the *Cincinnati Post*. He'd called me there several times in the past on the first Wednesday of the month. The guy never called at 6:30, when I always walked in the door. He always waited until 8:00, when he knew I'd had a couple of beers and a belly full of a good supper. That way maybe I'd let a little more slip than I would otherwise.

He tried to draw me out, and we ended up getting into an argument about what I could and could not tell him about the Ruppert case. It was an argument between friends, but I think I cussed him out and he cussed back. It was no big deal. But I couldn't even go to the FOP Lodge without the news hounds calling me up.

Right before I left the lodge, I got a tip from John Bohlen, the sheriff's major. Bohlen had an informant who told him Ruppert had lunch with the owner of Hamilton Coin and Antique (which sold guns and ammunition) last Thursday. Ruppert was asking this fellow about a silencer. I passed the word to Chief McNally, who was going to have a couple detectives check it out that night. I was anxious as hell to see if that was true. If it were, that would be another nail in the coffin.

I didn't watch myself on TV that night. I was tired of all that crap. I was at my office when the damn phone rang at 9:50 p.m. and I picked up the receiver and yelled: "It's ten till ten!" It was Paulette Ebbing, Glenn's wife, who told me she was worried that Glenn got off work at four o'clock and still wasn't home. I told her he had a hot lead on a murder case and was probably running that down. But I knew better. I knew he was getting himself full of juice someplace to wipe the memories of the last three days out of his mind.

At 10:45 p.m., Detective "Red Dog" Gabbard brought over a statement from a guy named Dean Cavett. Cavett owned the gun shop and used to eat with Ruppert at Frisch's and see him at the Hayden & Stone Brokerage.

Cavett said that a couple months ago, Ruppert mentioned something to him about a silencer for a gun, or firing a gun through a pillow to silence it. Then last Wednesday or Thursday, Cavett had to keep repeating himself to Ruppert when they were eating lunch at Frisch's. Ruppert explained he'd been down on the riverbank firing his .357 Magnum and couldn't hear very well. That made him a target shooter, just as we thought. The statement made me feel a hell of a lot better about this case. It kept getting better and better. You have two kinds of cases. The ones that start out real good and disintegrate in front of your eyes. And the other cases start out thin and build into something real good. This case was turning into the latter. The evidence for a conviction kept piling up.

At the police station that morning, I'd gathered all the detectives together. In my view, I told them, the case against Ruppert was shaping up well. His only out, I told them, was to plead not guilty by reason of insanity. The law in that regard required the burden of proof to be in the hands of the defense. In other words, the defense had to prove he was insane; I didn't have to prove he was sane.

"With eleven people going into the ground in this case, I'm going to hit him as hard as I can, and if he's insane, he's going to have to prove every damn inch of it," I said.

I instructed the detectives to interview all of Ruppert's neighbors, former schoolmates, employers, co-workers, friends and acquaintances, and get statements from them, hopefully showing that he was the most normal guy in town prior to Easter. That he never heard voices, never acted abnormally, always went to work on time, invested in the stock market, was an avid reader. I told them if somebody said he was a weirdo, or something like that, write that down, too. We weren't being tricky or cagey about it. It was my theory at that point that when Ruppert got to trial, his lawyers and psychiatrists were going to make him out to be nuttier than a fruitcake. And my job was to show, if I could, that he was normal, sane. Why in the world he committed this atrocious act, I did not know yet. But I was not going to give him the benefit of the doubt.

"A guy would have to be crazy to kill eleven members of his own family," my own secretaries told me.

But I could not even concede that. I had to keep looking for some motive, and whatever his reason was, I had to fight this thing and show that he was sane.

The detectives went to work looking up Ruppert's former associates and getting statements from them. Later that day, I took calls from the *London Sun* newspaper and *Newsweek* magazine. I was astounded that news of the case had reached that far. But I was bound by rules of the U.S. Supreme Court laid down in the Sam Shepherd murder trial, regarding fair trial verses free press. In other words, I was limited in what I could say.

Ruppert's preliminary hearing was scheduled for Friday, which I expected to be a circus, with all the press and spectators. I knew Holbrock and Bressler, Ruppert's attorneys, would go on a deep-sea fishing expedition to find out from my witnesses what my evidence was. I didn't want that to happen. So I scheduled a special session of the Butler County Grand Jury for Thursday—the same day as the Ruppert family funeral.

On Thursday morning, I presented the case to the Butler County Grand Jury. I had six or seven different law enforcement officers testify, and I outlined the law to the grand jurors on aggravated murder, murder, voluntary manslaughter, involuntary manslaughter, and negligent homicide. The Grand Jury voted at noon to return an indictment charging 11 counts of aggravated murder with a specification as to each count. The specification was that this was a purposeful killing involving the death of two or more persons as a result of a common course of conduct by the defendant. With this specification came the possibility of the electric chair.

As I left the grand jury room, the press descended with bright lights and television cameras. I told them grand jury proceedings were absolutely secret by law, and I couldn't comment directly or indirectly on anything regarding the grand jury. Of course, they were trying to get a story and didn't like that too much. So I went back to the office and sat down during lunch hour—what I called "dinner" when I was a kid. Anyway, I went over every word of that indictment to make sure it was absolutely correct. I had the secretary do it over again and had the foreman of the grand jury come back and sign it. I told the press the grand jury would report tomorrow at 9 a.m.

I watched the 11:00 news that night and saw those 11 caskets at the funeral service in the shape of a cross and heard the choir singing, and that really got to me. That got to me more than the sight of the dead bodies themselves. That night I saw little 4-year-old John in my mind again. I still could not shake him out of my head.

⬤ ⬤ ⬤ ⬤ ⬤

When I got to the office Friday, I called Gorman Clark of BCI and told him to look for a pillow with gun powder or nitrates on it, which may have been used as a silencer in the killings. Big surprise: Agent Todd found a pair of bloody pants and a shirt by Ruppert's dresser in his bedroom. I sifted through witness statements and police reports all afternoon and found some employment applications where Ruppert listed his hobby: "guns."

That night, I went out to the Don-Ron for a few cold beers with Howard "Cookie" Cook and Doug "BB" Johnson. We talked over some old cases and old stories. Then I went to Waldo's, which we called the "Sin Hole" because there was so much action down there, and met Ebbing. We drank a few beers and talked about the case. Then my kid brother, Tom, came in and gave me a dollar cigar to celebrate the birth of his baby girl, Laura. Tom's wife, Suzanne, had given birth to their first child that morning. She was seven pounds with long brown hair. That was the first dollar cigar I'd ever smoked. It was really good.

On my way home, I picked up a jumbo pepperoni pizza and two large Cokes from Richard's Pizzeria. My oldest son, Johnny, and I ate pizza and watched late movies on television, which we did every Friday night. It was a big thing for him. We always stayed up until two, three, or four o'clock in the morning, until I fell asleep in my chair. My wife learned a long time ago not to wake me when I fell asleep in my chair, because if I was tired enough to do that, I invariably cussed her out if she woke me up. Rather than hear my tirade, she always let me sleep in that chair until I woke up Saturday morning. But something else woke me; my phone rang at 1 a.m. It was Hugh Holbrock, Ruppert's attorney. He was at the Holiday Inn in Fairfield with a Dr. Mechanick, a famous psychiatrist and professor at the University of Pennsylvania. The reason for the call, Hugh said, was that his client was paranoid, extremely depressed and suicidal. They requested I take the necessary precautions to ensure his safety and post a guard to watch him 24 hours a day.

I spoke to Dr. Mechanick on the phone and asked how the massacre occurred. He relayed Ruppert's explanation. He told me Ruppert was carrying his guns down the stairs to go target shooting, when his brother, Leonard, asked him, "Will the rebate help the economy?"

Leonard was referring to the Tax Reduction Act of 1975, which would provide tax credits and rebates to middle-class Americans to help jump-start the economy.

Ruppert replied: "Not much."

The next question was about Ruppert's car.

"How's your Volkswagen running?" Leonard asked him.

According to Mechanick, Ruppert thought for years that Leonard had been sabotaging his car by ruining the points and plugs and either taking too much oil out or adding too much oil to the engine. Once, Leonard put his foot on the VW's bumper, and it fell off a week later.

Leonard's innocent question sent Ruppert into an uncontrollable rage, Mechanick told me. The imagined sabotage of the Volkswagen—along with Ruppert's belief that Leonard had reported him to the FBI as being a Communist, making it impossible for him to hold down a steady job—rushed through his mind.

In his rage, Ruppert shot Leonard. Then his mother lunged at him, and he shot her. Then he shot his brother's wife, Alma. He automatically started shooting the children, but didn't know why, according to Dr. Mechanick. Toward the end, he knew he had to finish them all off, so he put plenty of bullets in them to end the moaning and put them out of their misery.

Ruppert also believed his other lawyer, Joe Bressler, was betraying him. He didn't trust Bressler, because of an exchange he'd overheard at the police station, the psychiatrist told me. Bressler asked for coffee, and when Lt. Pater handed it to him, he said, "That'll cost you, brother." Bressler said: "OK. That's a deal." Ruppert interpreted that statement as Bressler's deal to betray him.

I arranged to meet Holbrock and the doctor at nine o'clock in the morning. Then I immediately called the jail and requested a guard be posted to watch Ruppert at all times. I also called Chief McNally at his house, got him out of bed, and relayed to him my conversation with Dr. Mechanick.

Johnny was asleep on the couch at that point, so I threw a blanket over him, turned off the TV, and went upstairs to bed.

* * * * *

After I woke up, I headed to Kosta's Restaurant, a diner on Court Street, as was my custom on Saturday mornings. I ordered a giant plateful of biscuits and gravy, hash browns and a slice of fried ham. I met my assistant Ed Lykins at the office and discussed the events of the previous night. I asked Ed to accompany me and take very good notes at the meeting with Holbrock and the psychiatrist.

According to Dr. Mechanick, Ruppert was grossly psychotic (and had been for the last 10 years), and suffered from a persecution complex and paranoia. It all started with an obscene phone call he'd made to a girl who worked at the local Lane Library. Among other things, he related that Ruppert was a little man who felt persecuted by the world. His motivation for committing the murders was notoriety, the doctor said. I asked the doctor why Ruppert didn't kill himself along with the others. Ruppert told the doctor he lay on the couch and looked at the ceiling and thought about killing himself for a couple of hours, but just couldn't bring himself to do it. Other things Ruppert told the doctor were that he shot the smallest boy, John, on the toilet, and that he considered the oldest boy to be a "son-of-a-bitch."

Hugh said he was giving us this information now, because they were going to enter a plea of not guilty by reason of insanity. They wanted the mental exams finished as soon as possible, because they were convinced Ruppert was insane and unable to stand trial. They wanted this wrapped up quickly, as there was no point in dragging it out for months. I agreed, and planned to have court-appointed psychiatrists examine Ruppert, along with a prosecution psychiatrist, Dr. Daniel Thomas, from Dayton.

Later that day, I consulted former prosecutor Dick Wessel about the case. He told me he'd give his right arm to be in it. He was like an old racehorse chomping at the bit when a big case came up. I had the greatest confidence, respect, and admiration for Wessel, and I consulted with him frequently. He was the most honest man I'd ever met. He was so honest, he sometimes made me feel uncomfortable, and I was an honest man. But that's the kind of fellow he was.

Dick advised me to take a hardline approach. He said he wouldn't be all that impressed just because some goddamn psychiatrist flew in on a jet from Philadelphia, looked at a guy for 45 minutes, and said he was nuts. In the meantime, we had hundreds of statements from people who knew Ruppert, saying that he appeared normal in every respect. That made a lot of sense to me, and that was what

I was going to do. If you take 11 lives, this prosecutor was not going to do you any favors. That's the way it had to be.

Next, attorney Jim Irwin came in. Jim lived a few doors down from Leonard and Alma Ruppert and their children, on Walter Avenue in Fairfield. He knew the Ruppert children very well. He sat down and told me some little stories about some of these children. Jim Irwin, who was one slick cookie, broke down and started crying. I was really impressed that Jim was so sensitive. I was also worried even more about my insensitivity to the murder scene.

Anyway, Jim Irwin told me he thought the best course of action, if I was convinced in my heart that the man was truly insane, was to wrap it up right then on the basis that Ruppert was incompetent to stand trial. Release Ruppert's full confession to the public so the community wouldn't think a mass slayer was at large, and let it go at that, Irwin advised.

I could see his thinking. That was the compassionate thing to do. But I was convinced that even if I had one doubt that this man was insane, I still had to prosecute him to the fullest extent of the law. I could not give him the benefit of the doubt.

I went home and shot baskets in my backyard all afternoon. I wanted to see if I could get my old eye back. In high school, I played varsity on the Hamilton High School Big Blue team, and we won the state championship that year. I didn't recapture any brief flashes of my former brilliance that afternoon in my backyard. All I got was a sunburned head and aching feet and legs.

A curious thing happened that week. I examined the photographs of the crime scene, and I noticed another Ruppert boy, David, who was 10 years old when he was gunned down. I was having trouble getting him out of my mind, too. So instead of having one of these dead children, little John, in my mind, I now had two of them in my head.

When I woke up Sunday morning, my feet, right arm and shoulder hurt so badly I didn't want to get out of bed. I thought I'd have to give up basketball. When I was able to get up, I went to the Train

Collectors meeting in Cincinnati and shopped around for the next addition to my train layout in my basement. I bought 12 model telephone poles for $1. I ran into Ernie Staley, a furnace man, who sold me a six-wheel steam switcher with a slope-back, bellringing tender, after we dickered around for a bit about price. I finally agreed to give him $75, which was pretty high, but that was the amount I usually parted with at those meetings. My shoulder still hurt when I got home, so I fell asleep in my big red chair in the TV room while watching the New York Knicks. I went to the office about six o'clock in the evening and continued working on the case.

Chapter 11

Until Easter Sunday 1975, most who knew James Urban Ruppert considered him a passive man who preferred to stay in the background. He was born in Wapakoneta, Ohio—best known as the birthplace of astronaut Neil Armstrong, who achieved fame as the first man to walk on the moon. But as Dick Perry wrote in the *Cincinnati Post* on June 18, 1975, "Ruppert reached only the treadmill of the everyday." Until Easter Sunday 1975, that is.

"He is described by some as a loner, but few speak ill of him," Perry wrote. "He could be a guy next door—polite, unassuming, and invisible."

James Ruppert had a sickly childhood. Diagnosed with bronchial asthma at age 2, he suffered lingering effects throughout his youth. He was unable to participate in gym class or go out for sports teams at his alma mater, Hamilton Catholic High School, where he graduated with few close friends in 1952. He also was hospitalized for spinal meningitis in his teens. His slight build and clean-cut look led others to consider him old-fashioned.

During Ruppert's childhood, his family lived in a barn-like structure without indoor plumbing, in Fairfield. His father, Leonard Sr., raised pigeons in half of the house. Leonard Sr. died when Ruppert was just 10. Family friends said Leonard Jr., the older brother, assumed the role of protector and surrogate father.

Investigator Jim Farquis met Ruppert his first day as a student at Hamilton Catholic High School in 1950. Farquis remembers Ruppert working at the school over the summer to prepare the classrooms for the upcoming academic year.

"He was kind of an ordinary guy," Farquis said. "He didn't bother anybody."

In high school, Ruppert shared a locker with Terry Malone, a popular student who would later coach football at Hamilton Catholic and

Badin high schools. Malone took the top half of the locker; Ruppert used the bottom half. In fact, Ruppert typically played the role of a social second-stringer, considered odd and a loner by most who knew him in high school. While older brother Leonard became a successful engineer and a respected family man, James dropped out of college after a couple years of night school at Xavier University and the University of Cincinnati. An average student, he earned Bs and Cs. He later worked at General Electric and as a draftsman for a temporary agency, traveling to different jobs around the Midwest. In his spare time, Ruppert enjoyed visiting the 19th Hole Cocktail Lounge, Hayden & Stone brokerage firm, Frisch's Restaurant, and the Lane Public Library.

"Everybody who went to the library knew who he was, because he went there every day," said librarian Joan Fatika. "He was a quiet person. He'd read books and newspapers."

At that time, the library displayed racks of daily newspapers—everything from the local publications to the *New York Times*, *Wall Street Journal*, and *Washington Post*.

"He would look at the financials," Fatika recalled.

Ruppert never displayed anti-social behavior in person, but once made an obscene phone call to a librarian. He typically refrained from conversation with library employees or other patrons, but always acknowledged them with a friendly but brief greeting.

"Nobody would ever suspect him of anything," Fatika said.

The day after the murders, all the library employees were stunned to see Ruppert's name in the newspapers.

"We were all shocked," Fatika said. "We were all calling each other and saying, 'Is that the person at the library?' No one could believe it."

When he left the library, he usually walked down the street to the brokerage house in the First National Bank Building to check on his stocks. Though he was obsessed with the stock market, he lost a hefty sum with his own investments. He drank at the 19th Hole about five nights a week.

Ruppert did excel at one activity: target shooting. As Vincent Isgro testified during the trial, Ruppert could "walk a can" with his rapid-fire shooting technique. Ruppert was suited up for shooting when Isgro saw him at a practice field about a year before the murders.

"He was wearing yellow shooting glasses, a gun belt, one holster and two pistols," Isgro testified. "It drew my attention. He was definitely shooting far superior than I was. He was chasing the can ... keeping it moving."

Ruppert employed those skills on Easter Sunday 1975, when he walked down the stairs of his mother's house, with his guns painstakingly loaded.

"He had a perfect view of everybody in the kitchen and living room," Farquis said. "He had them all down quickly."

Known on paper as No. 007909 at the Butler County Jail, Ruppert was housed in a first-floor, 6-by-8-foot holding cell after his arrest. The cell—A2—was sparsely furnished with a bunk, a small table, and an overhead light. The space typically was used to temporarily hold prisoners being booked into the jail, but Ruppert was moved there to allow constant observation by jail guards.

His routine never varied. He rose at 8 a.m. and was led to restroom facilities down the hall to shower and shave with an electric shaver. An assistant to his attorneys brought him fresh clothes for court appearances.

Guards said Ruppert liked to sleep and read. Newspapers and televisions were prohibited, but the defendant kept paperbacks, pocketbook editions and a Bible in his cell. He was partial to biographies. His reading material came from the jail library and his attorneys, and he liked to smoke a pipe as he read.

Though his only exercise was walking to and from the courthouse, Ruppert's weight held at 135 pounds during his stay at the jail. Deputies who transported him across the street for court proceedings said he remained silent. Only once did he speak, and that was to inquire about the score of a Cincinnati Reds baseball game.

Chapter 12

JOHN HOLCOMB
Monday, April 7 to Tuesday, April 8, 1975

One of my secretaries, Nancy Gersbach, who was in her early 20s and recently married, buzzed me to let me know Dick Perry was on the other line. She was a quiet girl, but damn competent.

"That Dick Perry is really crazy," Nancy said. "He's really nuts."

I asked why.

"He told me he had two questions: 'Number One: Do you wear a bra? And Number Two: Can I talk to Holcomb?'" Nancy said.

"What's the answer to Number One?" I asked her.

She hung up on me. I switched over to Dick Perry's line, and we conversed about this and that, but he mainly wanted to know when the arraignment would be. When we finished our conversation, Perry asked, "Incidentally, what's the answer to Number One?"

"Hell, I don't know," I said. "She hung up on me and thinks you're crazy."

I got back to work on the case. By then, I had separated all the information into categories. There were birth and death certificates for the victims; autopsy reports; scientific evidence that was starting to come back from BCI; and employment data on James Ruppert, which I found quite interesting. He was very highly regarded by his former employers. The only negative comment was that he was too slow and too meticulous in his work. I kept another file for the grand jury transcript, which I had the secretaries type up for the defense, in the interest of fair play and expediency. I also had documentary evidence showing Ruppert's financial holdings and promissory notes that he owed his brother and mother. Another file held police reports. The main file, and the most voluminous, was information to combat the psychiatric testimony in the case. This file held statements from people who knew Ruppert and claimed he was normal in every conceivable way. The only abnormal thing people said about him was that he was a loner and didn't go out with girls.

I had the police take some of Ruppert's hair, fingernail scrapings, clothes, fingerprints and palm prints without a search warrant and without his consent. In my view of the law, that was permissible. But I was sure this would be an issue at trial, and the defense would say I violated the defendant's constitutional rights. I kept a file for that purpose. And the final file contained a crime scene sketch and photographs of the bodies.

As I mulled the evidence over in my mind, I became more and more certain that Ruppert was sane. His behavior and his thinking were highly unusual, but he knew where he was, what he was doing, and could relate all the things he did. According to Ohio's legal test, those factors were sufficient to render him competent to stand trial. The test was whether the defendant was sufficiently sound of mind to understand and appreciate the nature of the charges against him, comprehend his situation, and furnish his counsel with the facts essential to the presentation of a proper defense. I thought Ruppert passed that legal test. Whether he knew the difference between right and wrong, or whether he had an irresistible impulse to commit these crimes, was a separate insanity issue, which would be decided at the trial, if it got that far. I left the office more convinced than ever that I would fight this thing as hard as I could.

I went home and watched the last three innings of the Reds 15-inning opener against the Dodgers. The Reds scored the winning run on an infield hit to the third baseman. Looked like the same old Reds. I had some terrible roast beef for supper and went back to work.

I decided then, that when the arraignment was over tomorrow, I would head down to Lexington's Keeneland Racetrack and watch some of those good horses run and drink some good, cold beer, for as long as my money held out. I'd have one of my secretaries lie about my whereabouts if anyone called for me.

The next morning, Tuesday, I looked out my office window and saw all the newsmen running back and forth across the street between the jail and courthouse, jockeying to secure a position to take Ruppert's picture when they brought him over for arraignment at 10:00. I had been at the office since 8:30 a.m. and was nervous as a cat, but it was a good nervous. It was the kind of nervousness I had before a big basketball game in high school. I called it pre-game jitters. I walked over to the arraignment at 10 till 10.

Chapter 13

Ruppert appeared at the Butler County Courthouse the morning of his arraignment, flanked by his attorneys and guarded by sheriff's deputies. His hands cuffed behind his back, he wore a jail-issue uniform and black-framed glasses.

Ruppert's lawyers entered pleas of not guilty and not guilty by reason of insanity. When asked to confirm his plea, Ruppert spoke in a barely audible voice: "Yes... yes."

Judge Fred B. Cramer ordered a psychiatric evaluation of Ruppert by the Butler County Forensic Center, to be conducted over the next 30 days. In light of the possible death penalty specifications, Cramer also ordered Ruppert held without bond.

A circus atmosphere reigned as Ruppert was escorted back to jail by deputies after the arraignment. Television camera crews and print photographers jumped in front of the defendant to capture his picture. Courthouse employees stuck their heads out of windows to catch a glimpse of the infamous defendant. And spectators lined Court Street to watch the drama unfold. Ruppert was the most hated man in Hamilton, and the town was obsessed with him.

In the three days following the mass murder, street sales of the *Hamilton Journal-News* nearly doubled. The Cincinnati newspapers also closely followed the story. In a feature published on April 9, 1975, *Cincinnati Post* reporter Ken Bunting described the "drama" and its "cast of characters." He called Holcomb the "chubby and balding" prosecutor whose favorite line to the media was, "No comment." McNally was the "tough, talkative, and candid" police chief who was "at his best talking in riddles off the record." Coroner Dr. Garrett Boone was a "grandfatherly type" who relished the spotlight "perhaps most of all." Boone was admonished by Judge Cramer for "too freely offering his opinions in interviews" and dramatically re-enacting for the media his theory of how the crime was committed. Defense attorneys Bressler and Holbrock were "walking contrasts." The younger, fashionable Bressler avoided the media, while the older Holbrock, considered "the best criminal lawyer in town," handled reporters with savvy, repeating the same lines over and over for each member of the press.

The case intrigued the national media, as well. The Ruppert murders made the front page of *The New York Times* and appeared inside *Newsweek Magazine*. The notoriety rivaled Hamilton's infamous Prohibition-Era "Little Chicago" days of gangsters, gambling, prostitution and speakeasies, when mobster John Dillinger holed up in a South Second Street house. In October 1933, Dillinger killed a sheriff and broke a fellow gangster out of a Lima, Ohio jail. When police homed in on Dillinger's Hamilton hideout, he had already slipped through their fingers.

The national media described Hamilton, population 68,000, as a suburb of Cincinnati, but its citizens begged to differ. This manufacturing city, with mills that churned out paper, vaults and automobile parts, had its own identity, a vibrant downtown business district, bedroom communities, Appalachian roots, and a storied past. And after 1975, it would forever be associated with the Ruppert murders.

Chapter 14

JOHN HOLCOMB
Tuesday, April 8 to Thursday, April 10, 1975

At the arraignment, Ruppert's attorneys entered pleas of not guilty and not guilty by reason of insanity on each count. I considered it a poor strategy on the part of defense counsel, because it gave me an opportunity to argue that the defendant was trying to take two bites out of the apple. He was, in effect, by his plea of not guilty, saying, "I didn't do it." And by his plea of not guilty by reason of insanity, he was saying, "But if you find that I did do it, then I was crazy."

Later that day, I received a tip that Jim Mense, a prominent insurance man in town, had received a letter from Ruppert requesting he visit him in jail. Mense went to the jail and described an odd visit with the defendant. He told me Ruppert asked him if he thought Holbrock and Bressler were competent lawyers. Mense answered in the affirmative. Ruppert then asked if Mense thought his lawyers would try to make a deal with the prosecutor. Mense replied he didn't think they would, unless it was in Ruppert's own best interest. Ruppert also asked Mense if he should bring in a nationally known criminal lawyer to handle his case.

Ruppert also told Mense he'd never been in any trouble before. "That may be," Mense replied, "but you're in big trouble now."

Mense said he felt compelled to ask Ruppert if he committed the murders, and Ruppert told him his lawyers advised him not to talk about that.

Ruppert appeared to be of sound mind during the conversation, Mense told me. Once or twice, the defendant even cautioned Mense to keep his voice down, so a deputy could not hear what they were saying. He and Ruppert and gone to high school together. When

Mense saw Ruppert at their class reunion eight or nine years before, and on the street on a few other occasions since, he'd always behaved appropriately, Mense said.

I knew the defense had Dr. Mechanick and might bring in another heavyweight from Boston, so I looked into the possibility of retaining one of the psychiatrists who testified in the Richard Speck trial. Speck was convicted of torturing, raping and murdering eight student nurses in their Chicago dormitory in July 1966. I expected to hear something back in a couple of days.

That night I needed to drive to the Greater Cincinnati Airport to pick up my mother, who was returning from visiting my youngest sister, Mary Sue, in North Carolina. I asked Ebbing to ride down with me. He told me to meet him at the Coachlite Inn down on Third Street, and we had a couple of quick beers before we drove to the airport. As I walked through the airport, I stopped at a newsstand and bought a copy of *Newsweek*. I saw a reference to the Ruppert case in there and saw my own name in the article. At once, I felt elation, or maybe vanity, because little Johnny Holcomb from Coralie Avenue in Hamilton had made *Newsweek* magazine. I also had this feeling that I must comport myself well from here on out, to avoid being a national goat. As these things ran through my mind, along with that image of little John Ruppert, I heard myself being paged over the airport loudspeaker. I panicked and imagined the worst. Did one of my children get hurt? Did something happen to my dad? So I went up to the Piedmont Airlines desk and asked what the message was, while Ebbing went to get my mother. They handed me a piece of paper with a name and a telephone number scrawled across it. "Call Dick Perry," it said.

That goddamn Perry, I thought. He was one reporter who would hound you to death. If you were on the toilet, he'd knock on the bathroom door to ask you a question. I called the number and Perry asked me if I was aware that Ruppert wrote a letter to a friend of his who was a public relations man from Mosler Safe Company. I told him I was aware, but had no other comment. I also proceeded

49

to tell him that he interrupted me at the airport and forced me to abandon an almost full beer on the airport bar. Perry just laughed and told me to hurry back there and maybe the beer would still be waiting for me. I went back to the bar to get my cold beer and, sure as hell, it was gone.

After we dropped Mom off, Glenn and I went back to the Coachlite for one beer. Then we went to Waldo's for another couple of hours while we discussed the case and drank a couple more beers. We agreed we had as many witness statements as we could get and would concentrate on getting additional school and employment records.

I got home around ten o'clock and handed the copy of *Newsweek* magazine to my wife. She was singularly unimpressed, being more impressed with the fact that I had been drinking beer and gotten home late. I went to bed.

On Wednesday morning I shaved, showered, and dressed for work. I made my way downstairs and saw my oldest son, Johnny, sitting at the kitchen table in his pajamas, eating a giant bowl of Cap'n Crunch, and reading the *Newsweek* magazine I'd brought home. He really was a smart kid and could read *Newsweek* easily, even though he was only 9. He didn't say anything, but I could tell he was thoroughly enjoying reading about his dad. I kidded around with my kids and tousled their hair, and Judy asked me if I wanted a piece of toast. That was about the best offer I ever got for breakfast: a piece of toast. Anyway, I took a couple swigs of orange juice straight from the bottle and headed out the door to work.

I read in *The Cincinnati Enquirer* that Hugh Holbrock was angry that his client didn't get a preliminary hearing. That told me he damn well wanted the Grand Jury testimony. I put Fran to work finishing up typing the testimony. She had taken time off for her husband's cartilage operation, but was back. I got a call from Karl Krucker of Dunlap's Clothing on Third Street, where I buy most of my clothes, telling me my raincoat was in. Krucker was about 75 years old and in perfect physical shape from walking to work a couple of miles each way every day of his life. He told me to send a good-looking girl over to pick up the coat. I told him I'd send a beautiful girl, so I sent my secretary Janet. She was a real knockout. She brought the coat back and told me Karl was funny and told her, "John has a lot of hot air, but he sure was right today."

Judge Cramer called and said he set the sanity hearing for Monday, May 12, and Tuesday, May 13. That told me something. A sanity hearing usually took half an hour. That told me Cramer had been in touch with the defense counsel and they told him about the heavyweight psychiatrist they had coming in and had gone into depth with him about what the psychiatrist would testify. I didn't even have any damned psychiatrists yet, so I prepared an entry to have one appointed from the Butler County Forensic Center. The whole case would turn on the sanity hearing and whether Ruppert was able to stand trial. Cramer also set June 16 for the beginning of the trial, should there be one.

As I opened my mail, I saw a photocopy of Senator Edward Kennedy being attacked by a segregationist mob in Quincy, Massachusetts. One of the guys attacking him in the forefront was a big-shouldered bald guy who really did look like me. A caption typed under the photo read, "Kennedy Attacked by Butler County, Ohio, Prosecutor John Holcomb." I recognized the font from the typewriters at the Hamilton Police Department. After you read a lot of police reports, you recognize the distinctive characteristics of the type. One of those goddamn guys typed this out and sent it to me.

These guys played tricks on me like that all the time. A few years back, Ebbing and his partner, Charlie Reid, made out a fake attempted suicide report on a girl I was representing in a divorce case. At the bottom, under "Reason For Attempted Suicide," it read, "She fell in love with her lawyer, John Holcomb, knew she couldn't have him, and therefore attempted suicide." They handed this thing to me with straight faces and stuck with their story for about an hour. I was so shaken I reached into my drawer for a tranquilizer, and that was when they started laughing. Anyway, that was the extent to which those guys would go to put a good one over on me. All in all, it made for a good feeling of camaraderie between the police and the prosecutor's office. They knew they could kid around with me, we could drink together, go to the racetrack together, come over and do work on my house, and I'd go help paint their houses. They were all really fine people.

I opened up the *Journal-News* later that afternoon and read a story about Ruppert sending out a letter to a prominent business-man to ask him if he should change lawyers. That was referring to Mense. It made me so mad I couldn't see straight. All of that stuff was highly prejudicial and played right into Holbrock's hands. I called John Bohlen over at the jail and chewed him out good. I planned to send a letter to Sheriff Carpenter, too.

A fellow named Bill Martin, chief prosecutor in the Richard Speck case, called to say he would line up three or four psychiatrists for me. He said you put them in a stable just like horses and then you run one out depending on the situation. He gave me some good ideas and strategies he used in the Speck case.

Working on this case day and night, my private practice was going to hell. This case could put me in bankruptcy if I didn't get some dough coming into my private practice between now and the end of June.

I opened up *The Cincinnati Post* at home later and read that some guy named Ken Bunting called me "chubby and balding" in an article he wrote. It made me madder than hell at first. I didn't worry about being bald, but to think the goddamn guy called me chubby. Hell, I wasn't chubby. But on the other hand, I supposed he could have called me fat, so maybe he did me a favor. One thing I planned to do before this trial was trim down a little bit. That was one of my resolutions. All these late hours and hustling around was bound to peel some off.

Judy and the kids came trooping in the back door. John had a certificate from the Y saying he'd graduated to the "Minnow Class" in swimming, and Mary Ann had one saying she'd graduated to the "Polliwog Class." Andy and Jeff didn't have any certificates. I guessed they were still in the wading pool. I asked Judy what was for supper, and she said ground beef. I asked where it was, and she said it was in the freezer.

"Well, hell with it," I said. "I'll just go back to work."

I told her I had had a late lunch and would be OK. If I told her I was going to eat someplace else, it would have offended her, so I didn't tell. But I went down to Tom's Cigar Store on Main Street and bought five copies of *Newsweek*. That was the vanity in me. Then I went next door to the Homestead (known for serving the best shredded beef sandwiches around) and got two fish sandwiches with mustard and a large Pepsi to go. I took my food to the office and worked on the case some more. During the course of the night, I had four Pepsis. That was what was putting the fat on me, and it had been all my life. I if cut out the Pepsi and beer, I'd be trimmed down real nice by trial time, I thought.

As soon as I got to the office Thursday—first shot out of the box—Dick Wessel came through the door with yesterday's *Cincinnati Post*. He had underlined in red the words "balding and chubby." I knew I was really going to take a shellacking over that. The girls in the office looked at it. Sharon laughed so hard she couldn't stand it. Nancy said she thought it was unkind. Janet said she didn't think I was balding and chubby. Fran wasn't there yet.

I got to work lining up my psychiatrists. I selected Dr. Daniel Thomas in Dayton, and he recommended a classmate who was at North Carolina University, if we needed another doctor. Then I called the DA's office in Philadelphia trying to get a line on Dr. Mechanick. To my surprise, they had never heard of him. They said they'd get some information and call me back. I also placed a call about Dr. Ames Robey, in Ann Arbor, Michigan. I figured if he was connected with the University of Michigan, that would make a hell of an impression on Judge Cramer, because that's where he went to school. My immediate objective was to get Ruppert to trial, rather than having him shipped off to the Lima State Hospital as being incompetent to stand trial.

I sent Ebbing to Lane Library to get a complete list of titles and authors Ruppert had checked out in the last several years. The police also took books out of his house, so I told Ebbing to bring me those, too. I looked at Ruppert's high school transcripts, which showed he was an average student. He had an IQ of 116, which landed one point above the average range of 85 to 115. So the guy wasn't a genius (that would be a 160 IQ), or even in the high IQ range of 140.

Chapter 15

As expected, the press came out in full force, along with about 25 spectators, for Ruppert's two-day competency hearing May 12 and 13. Three psychiatrists and one psychologist testified in Judge Fred Cramer's courtroom. All believed Ruppert to be competent to stand trial, in spite of his mental health issues.

Dr. Howard Sokolov, of the Butler County Forensic Center, testified that he detected signs of a "paranoid psychotic state" in the defendant. Under cross-examination by the defense, he stipulated that Ruppert had spinal meningitis in 1953, which can produce brain damage, but said he saw no evidence of that in the defendant.

Dr. Dan Thomas testified that Ruppert was capable of standing trial, did not suffer from mental illness, but did have a paranoid personality. Dr. Victor Thaler agreed that Ruppert had a paranoid personality, but also saw schizoid traits. Ruppert did not relate deeply to people and was a loner, he said.

Dr. Robert J. McDevitt testified that Ruppert suffered from a form of paranoid psychosis, feelings of persecution, and a misinterpretation of reality. He told the court about the defendant's belief in a conspiracy against him.

The defense did not call any of its own witnesses, but asserted during cross-examination that their client's inability to trust his own attorneys impaired his ability to participate in his own defense, making him incompetent to stand trial.

After the testimony, Judge Cramer found Ruppert competent to stand trial.

While making his ruling, Cramer noted that the presence of mental illness in a defendant is insufficient to preclude him or her from standing trial. Under Ohio law, a suspect is competent to stand trial if a preponderance of evidence shows the defendant is capable of understanding the nature and objective of the proceedings against him or her and is capable of assisting in the defense. Cramer ruled Ruppert met those criteria.

Cramer set the trial date for June 16, 1975. Ruppert could opt for a jury of 12 peers or a three-judge panel to decide his fate. A prospective pool of 75 jurors was drawn shortly after the conclusion of the competency hearing.

After the hearing, Alma Ruppert's mother approached the prosecution table in the courtroom. She was deeply distraught that she had not been notified until four o'clock in the morning that her daughter, son-in-law, eight grandchildren, and friend Charity had been murdered. The bodies were discovered at 9:45 p.m., but she was not informed until six hours later. She was appalled that even the crowd of strangers that gathered in the street knew about the murders before she did. Prosecutors told her that the police notified her as quickly as they were able to ascertain her relationship to the victims, but she remained troubled. She wanted to go to the jail, confront James Ruppert, and show him the photographs from the funeral. She thought it might have some effect on the man she once considered a friend. Due to jail protocol, and much to Edna Allgeier's distress, that meeting would never take place.

Chapter 16

John Holcomb
Friday, May 30 to Tuesday, June 3, 1975

Dr. Charles Feuss examined Ruppert at the jail for about an hour and a half. His preliminary impression was that Ruppert was a paranoid schizophrenic, much more paranoid than schizophrenic, and at the very most would be considered borderline psychotic. He also felt that on the date in question, Ruppert knew the difference between right and wrong and had the ability to hold to the right and resist the wrong, if he had so desired.

The autopsy report, more than 50 pages, documented a total of 40 bullet wounds in the 11 victims. There were 26 bullets found. The victims were not piled up on top of each other, no furniture was knocked over, no blood splattered on furniture. It was almost as if they had been sitting on the floor and simply fell over.

The trajectory of some of the bullets was at a 30- to 40-degree angle, consistent with the theory that Ruppert was standing over several of the victims while they were sitting down, possibly on the floor. The oldest boy, Lenny, was more than six feet tall and was shot at least twice in the chest, with bullets angled upward. He had been shot while standing up. Ruppert's brother was also standing up when he was shot.

On Saturday, I was able to take a break from the gruesome details that filled my mind. Working on model trains in my basement always helped me unwind. Two friends (my kids called them the "Train Men") came over to rewire my O-gauge layout. We all worked on it for about five hours, which relaxed me and dried up the sweat in the palms of my hands, so to speak. We had all of the track down and most of the switches connected. Both of the two main lines were operating. One more five-hour session, and we'd have all the switches wired up and my switchyard connected into it.

I wanted to see the Freedom Train when it passed through Middletown that Tuesday, so I took my little son Jeffrey and my nephew Mark, who was 4 years old. The train was powered by a steam locomotive, a former Reading Railroad steamer. That train was three hours late. Talk about why the railroads went out of business.

We went to a gun shop on Central Avenue and then got ice cream cones. Jeffrey and Mark got it all over themselves, so when we walked back to the railroad station, I was holding two sticky hands. But I enjoyed it nevertheless.

When we finally heard the whistle in the distance, this amazing old locomotive bellowing out black smoke roared around the bend like a thunderstorm on rails. It traveled maybe 15 or 20 mph at the most. But it seemed like it was going 100 mph. As it rounded the bend, the engineers laid into the whistle as it passed the railroad station and flashed its headlight. That old engine made a terrific roar as it passed by. Nothing is as loud as a steam locomotive.

Mark started to cry, but Jeff was more amazed than afraid. We all waved to the four or five old-timers in the cab of this locomotive. They wore bib overalls and old-time engineer caps. A couple wore goggles. They were having the time of their lives, waving to the crowd, and were probably brought out of retirement to run that steamer.

It was worth the three-hour wait.

Chapter 17

John Holcomb
Monday, June 2 to Saturday, June 14, 1975

We had about 500 pieces of evidence so far. We needed to meet with the BCI agents to establish the chain of evidence, or in other words, to trace each piece from where the agent picked it up to its final destination at the BCI lab.

Glenn Ebbing and Officer Leroy Henes drove to the crime lab in London, Ohio, with me. On the way, I got pulled over on Interstate 71 by the highway patrol. You've never seen three badges appear from inside billfolds so fast in your life. They told us we were caught speeding by the State Highway Patrol airplane. When we told them what our hurry was and they sent us on our way without writing us a ticket or even giving us a warning. The officer told me he read about the case and wished me luck on it.

The BCI identified the bullets fired from the Astra .22 revolver, the Sentinel revolver, and the .357 Magnum. Leroy asked why we'd brought him along on this trip, since he had not been involved in the case at all. I told him he would make a fine detective one day, since he realized his presence seemed extraneous. I explained that we were stopping at Scioto Downs Racetrack in Columbus on the way back, and he was going to drive us home from there.

But it turned out to be a stroke of luck that Leroy went with us. He made a significant observation about the evidence, based on the slides we watched at BCI. He noticed that Ruppert's rifle carrying case was open and leaning against his bedroom wall. If he were about to go target shooting, as he claimed, why take the rifle out of its case before going downstairs? There was also a gun box on his dresser for the Astra. Wouldn't he have carried the Astra in the gun box to go target shooing? He wasn't going to go target shooting with two loaded guns tucked inside his waistband, a handgun in one hand and a rifle in the other. That was ridiculous. He would have brought the guns down in their cases if his plan was to shoot targets. I was going to try my damnedest to show he never had any intention of target shooting that day.

At the harness races, I lost the first eight races, but hit one on the last race of the day, so it ended on a happy note. On the way home, I fell asleep before we even got out of the parking lot, with Leroy behind the wheel.

The next day I worked on subpoenas for 64 prospective witnesses. I put them out in several batches—first the 20 police officers who participated in the investigation; then the psychiatrists and psychologists; then the insurance, benefit, estate and probate experts; and last, the rebuttal witnesses. These were relatives, friends of the family and acquaintances of Ruppert from the Hayden-Stone stock brokerage, the 19th Hole Cocktail Lounge, and from Frisch's, where he ate lunch nearly every day. They all said he seemed completely sane.

I wanted to get these prepared in advance, before my secretaries Fran and Mary Sue left for the summer. That was part of my arrangement with them. They were both so good at their jobs, they could write their own tickets. While they both stayed home with their families for the summer, I brought in two college girls to take their places. I sure hated to see them go; they were both crackerjacks. Mary Sue worked like a machine and Fran was my confidant and sounding board. I was sure as hell going to miss them.

* * * * *

Later that week, Ebbing drove the same route the Leonard Ruppert family took the day of the murders. When they left from the Allgeier house and drove to 635 Minor Avenue, Alma's mother said they always traveled by way of River Road. It was 10.9 miles, and it took Ebbing 25 minutes traveling at the speed limit. If this was the case, and it certainly was, if Leonard Ruppert left the Allgeier house at 4:30 p.m., as Mrs. Allgeier said, they arrived at Minor Avenue at roughly five o'clock. They had an Easter egg hunt in the yard, which took a little time. So this killing occurred right around six o'clock, just as the coroner said.

I went over the autopsy reports with Dr. Boone and Dr. Swinehart at Mercy Hospital. I planned to have Dr. Swinehart use some diagrams prepared by Dr. Boone's son, who was an art instructor at Earlham College in Indiana. He prepared some blank diagrams of the human body and Swinehart located the positions of the bullets and wounds for each of the victims. We knew from BCI that 44 bullets were fired, and 40 of them hit the victims. Of those 40 hits, 38 were lethal, according to Dr. Boone.

Dr. McDevitt's opinion was that Ruppert was psychotic with regard to the killing of his mother and brother, but he was much less certain with regard to the other nine. Ruppert said he liked his nieces and nephews and did not consider them part of the conspiracy against him. The guy sure as hell wasn't helping my case by saying Ruppert was psychotic, and that was going to be a really big problem at trial. I knew Judge Cramer put a lot of faith in what Dr. McDevitt said. McDevitt did say that Ruppert was very clever, very organized, and entirely capable of formulating a plot such as this and carrying it out. McDevitt also said if he had seen Ruppert the day before the massacre, he would not have considered his condition severe enough for hospitalization. He would have treated him as an outpatient.

Dan Fischer told me he wanted to participate in the case, the biggest murder in the history of this area, but he had no criminal experience. So I needed some more help. I picked Mike Gmoser, who had been on my staff since January and was a young man with a bright future. He was smart, but best of all, he loved to work. He was the only assistant prosecutor I'd ever seen—outside of myself— who would go to the prosecutor and ask for more work. The hardest working prosecutor I'd ever seen was Dick Wessel. He worked like a dog, and was conscientious and hard working. But Mike Gmoser was really a worker, too, so I hired him as a three-quarter time assistant and gave him a $5,000 raise, which put him up to $14,000 a year.

I put Mike to work right away on this case. For four days that week, Mike, Dan and I spent all day and night getting witnesses together from the General Electric Corporation in Cincinnati and Schenectady, New York, to verify the existence of insurance policies on Leonard's life. The lawyer handling the estate for the Ruppert family couldn't wait until the damn case was over to open the estate and send off all the insurance policies, so they were all processed and were at several different insurance companies around the United States. We couldn't come up with the originals of these policies, so the best evidence rule required that we come up with certified copies and have a witness with the certified copy attest that it was a record kept in the regular and ordinary course of business. That's why it took so long getting those witnesses lined up.

Fischer went out with Ebbing, and Gmoser went out with Red Dog Gabbard, to talk to the witnesses once again. We had all kinds of statements from the witnesses, and their testimony would be two or three weeks away. I wanted to make sure our witnesses hadn't forgotten what they'd said, and I also wanted to find out whether the defense had investigators out talking to them, trying to get them to change their stories.

Every day during the week before the trial we worked until 2 a.m. I'd been walking to work that week to relieve my tension. Fischer had been walking to work, too. Gmoser was the only one of us who had a car with him on Thursday night, and it was a little Corvette. He gave us a ride home in that little thing. Fischer and I are big and heavy, and the three of us piled into that little Corvette, which makes a heck of a lot of noise, and pulled up in front of my house. I suspected the neighbors saw me roll in at 3 a.m., all of us piled into this Corvette laughing, and they said, "Yep, here comes the prosecutor in again at 3 a.m. He's out partying, drunker than hell, with a big murder case starting Monday." Sure as hell, I bet you that's what they thought. Nobody but a nut would work that late on a weeknight. If they think Ruppert's crazy, what about me?

Chapter 18

When Mike Gmoser joined the prosecution team, one of his first tasks was painstakingly going through the house at 635 Minor Avenue and taking an extensive inventory of pertinent items. Because the scene remained preserved for the trial, dried blood still covered the surfaces.

"The house was like a dried scab," Gmoser said. "It had a musty odor."

The blood and odor were sharply juxtaposed with the memorabilia of a typical family home: the grandchildren's Easter baskets, animal knickknacks, a metal cake carrier on a marble-topped table, a partially filled coffee cup, an ashtray with a few stubbed-out cigarette butts, a *TV Guide*, live greenery, a book on how to grow better house plants, white crocheted doilies and newspapers.

"It showed a peaceful place," Gmoser said. "An ordinary home and ordinary memorabilia that make a house a home, and all of that in contrast with the horrific scene the first responders found."

Another significant item found in the house was a book on psychology and paranoid schizophrenia. The prosecution team thought Ruppert read that book to educate himself on aspects of mental illness, pointing to premeditation.

"That gave you an insight into his mental processes," Gmoser said. "The challenge was always to prove he met the threshold to know right from wrong. To us, it was a hatred he had for the brother who had it all, had the kids, had the love of the mother. And, he was losing his ass in the stock market."

The hollow-point bullets used in the killings also showed premeditation, Gmoser said. That type of bullet, unlike those commonly used for target shooting, mushroomed upon impact with tissue, inflicting maximum damage, and causing immediate incapacitation.

Most horrifyingly, Gmoser saw evidence in the house that the children's final moments were filled with terror, desperation and attempts to evade the barrage of gunfire rained upon them by their uncle.

"My most vivid memory was seeing the walls in which there were fingernails embedded into the plaster, where the kids were trying to climb the walls to escape," Gmoser said.

Chapter 19

JOHN HOLCOMB
Sunday, June 15, 1975

It was the day before the trial. I'd gotten a decent night's sleep for the first time in a month, so I took my son John out to the farm. We met my brother, Tom, there. Right away, Tom let John do a little target shooting with a 9-millimeter, and that made his day. I squeezed off five shots with it myself, but didn't hit the target. Then Tom took John down to the big pond we have on the farm, and they fished for about three hours. I didn't join them. I just walked around a little, then sat down on a stump and thought about the case. I hadn't had my mind off it for a long time. Just being outside on the farm relaxed me. When we got back to the house, I watched the Reds lose to the Cubs, 4-3, then went back to the office to prepare my opening statement.

At five minutes till midnight, my opening was finished. I was ready to go to trial—as ready as I'd ever be. Of course, my rebuttal witnesses weren't ready yet. I would be doing that at night, as the trial progressed, because they wouldn't be needed for two weeks. But otherwise, I was ready.

Ruppert had opted for a three-judge panel to hear his case instead of a jury of his peers. After my opening statement in the morning, the three judges that would hear the case would tour the crime scene. It was June, and it was hot, and the storm windows were still on that house. I knew that when they walked through, they were going to suffocate and gag from the stench. I hoped it was hot, and I hoped it stank, especially so Judge Cramer got a real good whiff of it. That would make it more realistic to him in his ivory tower. Maybe he'd still have a whiff of that in his nostrils when he pondered some of the novel questions sure to be raised in this case.

Judge Cramer's presence on the panel scared me to death. He was probably the smartest judge this county ever had, one of the smartest in the country, I'd say. It was a pleasure to try a case in front of him. He was brilliant and really knew his stuff. But he was lenient. He loved novel questions and metaphysical questions—and loved to strain on a word.

I wasn't worried about Judge Robert Marrs. He was a former prosecutor. Of course, nobody had ever seen a case like this, but Judge Marrs had a realistic approach to criminal justice. Not to say that he was unfair—he was fair—but he was a no-nonsense judge. He was a prosecutor's judge. He had a no-nonsense air about him.

The third judge, Arthur Fiehrer, was a good, solid, middle-of-the-road judge. I knew he had recently found several people to be not guilty by reason of insanity, and I was sure that's why the defense wanted him on the case. But I wasn't worried about him. He was a solid guy. One thing about the Fiehrer family: they were a bunch of brothers, and one had worked as a lawyer and assistant prosecutor for 17 years before he died. The others were businessmen. They came from more or less humble beginnings, and all made successes of themselves. I'd never met a Fiehrer who didn't have common sense and wasn't a complete gentleman in every sense of the word.

So I thought about the judges as I readied myself to try this case, knowing they would have to tour that scene. And as I thought about the scene, it took me back to that night, Easter Sunday 1975, at 635 Minor Avenue. I would never forget that. I remembered Leonard Ruppert's black Chevy van parked in front of the house. Parked in front of it was a gray Volkswagen Beetle that belonged to Jim Ruppert, Leonard's brother, the defendant. It was chilly, the temperature in the 30s. We took a picture of the thermostat in the house, which showed it was 72 degrees inside. I walked in the front door and the first thing I saw was, strangely enough, a green Easter basket with yellow carnations in it on a stand. Under that stand in blue slacks, black and white saddle oxfords, and a blue and yellow plaid smock lay Ann Delores Ruppert, age 12, with four bullet holes in her head, sprawled in a puddle of blood with her glasses knocked halfway off her face.

Moving around the room counterclockwise, there was a couch to the left with a coffee table in front of it. Between the couch and coffee table lay Lenny, age 17. He wore the type of high-top boots all the teenagers wore and had on blue slacks and a blue long-sleeve shirt.

Between Lenny and his brother, Mike—Michael James Ruppert, age 16—there was a little footstool. Mike lay on the floor next to it. Moving around the room, on a beige or grayish carpet with a red rose design, there was a couch on the opposite wall, and on that couch was a blanket or a quilt and a pillow. On the floor, right in front of that couch was little Johnny Ruppert, age 4. The poor little fellow wore a little knit shirt with football designs on it, corduroy pants and black and white tennis shoes. At his feet was a *TV Guide* and right next to his hand was that chocolate Easter egg in a pink tinfoil wrapper. He was lying on his left side looking at the floor, with a bullet hole in the side of his head. I told myself: "Johnny, I'll never forget you as long as I live; I hope I can do you justice."

Moving toward a desk directly next to the front door, I saw Tommy Ruppert, age 15. Tommy had been shot in the head and was staring out into nothing. His glasses were knocked down around his mouth. He had on a white shirt with a green lengthwise design on it, a pair of Levis and a pair of work shoes. On the coffee table were two revolvers. On the arm of the couch in the living room was a third revolver. Moving toward the kitchen, I saw Leonard Rudolph Ruppert Jr., age 42, wearing dark blue pants with a black belt, and a white shirt with a yellow and green design in it. He had been shot in the back, as well as a number of times in the head.

Moving into the kitchen and going clockwise, I saw a little girl—Theresa Ruppert, age 9—with blue and white tennis shoes on, blue and white plaid slacks, and a blue knit shirt with white stripes. She, too, was shot in the head. Her mother's foot was in her face.

Moving clockwise, I saw the mother, Alma Ruppert, with her glasses still on. She wore a dark blue skirt and white long-sleeve blouse. She was actually lying in blood, as she had been shot in the chest. She was next to the stove. Moving clockwise toward the refrigerator, I saw David Scott Ruppert, age 11. Oh my God, his face was in a pool of blood three feet in diameter. He wore a pink tee shirt, blue pants and black and white tennis shoes. Next to his feet, leaning against the refrigerator, was a Marlin rifle. My God, David looked so much like my 9-year-old son, John, when he was sleeping. In the pool of blood next to his head, I saw a quarter. Rest in peace, Dave.

On the other side of the refrigerator was Grandmother Charity. She had on pink slacks and a white blouse with a pink sweater. Her mouth was open, and she was staring at the ceiling. Her glasses were off to the left, and she had really been blasted in the chest. She had been blasted right in the heart, I could guarantee you.

Close to the back door, I saw Carol Diane Ruppert, age 13, also lying in a pool of blood. She had been shot at least three times in the left side of her head. She had on white tennis shoes, blue Levis and a white T-shirt with a little wristwatch on her left wrist. All the shots to her head had been very close together, and blood was starting to drain out the back door. She was the closest to escaping, but not close enough.

That was my memory of touring the house. There was nothing more left to say about it. I'd worked hundreds of hours on this case. I wasn't complaining; it was my job and I loved my job and tried to do it the way it ought to be done. I sought no accolade for it. It was just a statement of fact. I'd put hundreds of hours on it, cheating my children by not being home, cheating my wife by being sharp tempered and short with her. It had strained my relationship with my wife, and I certainly hoped that would change when all this was over. She didn't understand what I'd been going through, why I was so short with her, or why I cussed her out.

I'd thought about it a whole lot. I'd considered and analyzed what the doctors had to say. In my heart, I believed James Ruppert, in his twisted way (not legally insane, but in his own twisted way) plotted and planned and set up the murder of his entire family so he could inherit their assets (close to $300,000 worth) and use it as his stock market money. I honestly believed it.

And I knew this. He killed 11 people without any excuse. He wiped out the equivalent of 600 years of human existence. That's what the remaining life span of those 11 people would have been. There was no justification for it, no excuse for it. Now I was into it. I'd done the best I could up to this point, and I was going to do the best I could for the next three or four weeks that this trial lasted.

"Jimmy Ruppert—you whining, sniveling, yellow little son-of-a-bitch—you belong to me," I thought, with every ounce of sincerity in body.

That was it for the night. It was a quarter past midnight, and I was due in court at 9 a.m.

Chapter 20

Exactly 32 minutes before James Ruppert's trial was to begin on Monday, June 16, 1975, the electricity went out in the Butler County Courthouse. One of the judges, some reporters and a handful of curiosity-seekers were trapped in the elevator until a few of the riders were able to pry open the doors from the inside. Judge Fiehrer stepped off the elevator and climbed the stairs to the third-floor courtroom where the trial would be held, while a crowd of spectators remained in the dark first-floor lobby. Electricity was restored about 15 minutes later.

The trial was the hottest ticket in town. Spectators stood along Court Street to catch a glimpse of Ruppert being led into the courthouse. Others lined up outside Judge Cramer's courtroom early so they could get a seat. When they finally were allowed in, they filled the courtroom to capacity. Members of the press sat in the jury box, which was empty due to Ruppert's request for a three-judge panel to hear his case.

Ruppert, wearing dark-framed glasses, a striped shirt, and a solemn face, was led to the defense table as photographers clicked away. Attorney Hugh Holbrock asked them not to take photographs of his client in handcuffs, and they complied.

Judge Cramer cautioned that he would not tolerate any outbursts or comments of any kind from the audience, and instructed spectators not to exit the courtroom while the trial was in progress. About 10 minutes after the proceedings began, Cramer announced the judges would tour the crime scene. Ruppert leaned and whispered something in Holbrock's ear. Holbrock then announced that his client did not wish to tour the house. The three judges left the courthouse and traveled to 635 Minor Avenue, while Ruppert was taken back to his cell to wait.

Outside the Minor Avenue residence, another crowd had gathered. About 50 people waited to watch the events unfold. The house's front and back doors had been boarded up with plywood and "No

Trespassing" signs. Two officers pried off the covering over the front door and placed it to the side. News reporters were allowed inside, but only for five minutes. They climbed the three-step stoop and entered under the small, scalloped, metal awning.

"One thing that stood out in my mind forever was, it was so hot and so stuffy, and there was dried blood everywhere," said *Journal-News* reporter Nancy Baker. "One of the judges picked up a quarter, and there was dried blood on it. There were bullet holes everywhere."

The sloppy joes from Easter dinner remained in the skillet. Everything was exactly the way it had been on Easter Sunday. The house stank.

After the tour, judges and members of the media returned to the courtroom for opening statements. First up, Prosecutor Holcomb painted Ruppert as a greedy, manipulative, cold-blooded killer obsessed with guns and money. He claimed the evidence would show the defendant, an unemployed draftsman with financial problems, planned and carried out the heinous crime to become sole heir to $300,000 in life insurance payouts and the estates of his brother, mother, sister-in-law, nieces and nephews.

Ruppert had only $2,600 in assets, and carried debts of $4,500, which he owed to his mother and brother. His brother, Leonard, on the other hand, was a successful engineer with a healthy savings account, a good job, a wonderful family, a nice home, and substantial insurance policies.

James Ruppert had three "abiding interests" in life: avidly reading books about psychology and psychiatry, shooting alternating guns in rapid-fire succession and playing the stock market, Holcomb said. Shortly before Easter, Ruppert had asked a friend about a silencer.

"Ruppert planned, calculated, and designed" to "obliterate" his entire family, then plead insanity as part of his "master plan," Holcomb argued. If his sinister plan succeeded, Ruppert would to be sent to Lima State Hospital for the Criminally Insane "until such time as the psychiatrists determine he has been restored to reason, and he would walk out a free man with $300,000 in his pocket," the prosecutor argued.

On the day of the massacre, as his unsuspecting family socialized after an Easter egg hunt, Ruppert calmly walked down the stairs with three loaded revolvers and a rifle. He fired off 21 shots—"lighting fast, as only a marksman could do," Holcomb said—rendering the 11 adults and children either dead or incapable of fleeing the first floor of the house.

The defendant then "coolly and deliberately" reloaded three times and continued his assault, delivering a coup de grâce to nine of the victims. He first reloaded a nine-shot gun and emptied it into his relatives. Then he reloaded nine more shots, again firing those into his family members. Finally, Ruppert reloaded nine additional shots, and fired five of those bullets into the victims. Of the 44 shots he fired, 40 hit their mark and 38 of those inflicted lethal wounds. No shots had been fired from the rifle, which leaned against the refrigerator as backup in case someone made it out of the house and tried to run away. Ruppert waited three hours, "to make sure they were absolutely dead," before he cleaned up, changed clothes and called police, Holcomb added.

The defense made no statement, reserving the right to deliver its opening remarks after the prosecution presented its case.

Officer Robert Minor, the first law-enforcement official on the scene, was the prosecution's initial witness. He described seeing a calm and collected Ruppert in the doorway at 635 Minor Avenue, as bodies sprawled on the living room floor behind him. Other witnesses included Glenn Ebbing and BCI agents. The agents testified that three handguns had been fired, but the rifle found leaning against the refrigerator had not. Ruppert's fingerprints were found on one of the handguns and a box of .22-caliber ammunition in the house, and his hands tested positive for nitrates from burning gunpowder. In an upstairs bedroom, trousers were found that contained minute specks of Type-O blood-covered gunpowder. Ruppert had type B, but the victims had types O and A. A shirt was found on the bedroom dresser, and a rifle case hung from a closet door. Also recovered from the house was a small book titled *Dictionary of Psychology*, found in the living room.

Deputy coroners testified that all the victims had been shot multiple times, except Alma and little John, who were shot only once. Charity, 65, suffered three bullet wounds to her head and chest; Leonard Jr., 42, five to his head, abdomen, and chest; Leonard III, 17, six to his thorax and chest; Michael, 16, two to his chest; Thomas, 15, three to his head and abdomen; Carol, 13, six to her head, chest, and abdomen; Ann, 12, four to the head; David, 11, six to the thorax and head; Teresa, 9, three to the head and chest; John, 4, one to his head; and Alma, 38, one to the chest, which pierced her heart. Coroners placed the time of death at roughly 6:00 p.m., give or take half an hour.

During the entire day of testimony, Ruppert showed no emotion, but sat calmly and quietly at the defense table.

Chapter 21

John Holcomb
Monday, June 16, 1975

I dreamed about the case, vividly, all night long, and woke up feeling strangely refreshed. I thought about every word I would say in my opening statement and the way I would say it. After showering and shaving, I heard a free-for-all down in the kitchen. Little Andy and little Jeffrey were throwing their cereal on each other and generally raising hell. Then, lo and behold, wonder of all wonders, Judy asked me if I wanted some breakfast. I told her a few pieces of bacon would do. I jammed it down and headed to the office. I was the first one there.

I had sweaty hands—pregame jitters—but aside from that, I felt pretty good. I met Dan and Mike over at the courthouse, and we took our places at the prosecution table. All of a sudden, all the photographers ran up and started taking our pictures and turned the TV lights on. I remember feeling how phony it was. How are you supposed to act when all those lights are on you? You can't crack jokes, because prosecutors aren't supposed to do that. So you try to pick out a spot on the wall and stare stonily ahead, trying to look tough.

I looked across the courtroom, and Ruppert was staring at a fixed spot on the floor. Hugh Holbrock sat at the middle of the table, laughing and carrying on. Joe Bressler had his head down, somber and sober. When court convened, Judge Cramer announced the tour of the premises would occur first. I sent Mike and Dan and stayed behind to get the physical exhibits lined up to facilitate their presentation. We had 101 exhibits. It would have been twice that number if some of them had not been combined.

When the judges returned, I made my opening statement. The very first sentence out of my mouth, I referred to an "eleven-account indictment," instead of an "eleven-count indictment." From that point on, I was OK. If I do say so myself, I gave a hell of a good opening statement. I put this thing in the perspective that it needed to be in: Ruppert planned and carried out the murders for the sole purpose of inheriting his family's $300,000 estate.

That day, we got all of our BCI and police-related physical exhibits out of the way. We had all the bullets, blood and fingerprints matched up, the crime scene photographs and the diagrams. The thing that impressed me most of all when the day was over: All the guys from BCI—the real pros, the experts, the criminologists, crime specialists, scientists—shook hands with me and said I did a hell of a job. They said they were glad to come down here anytime, under any circumstances, because they liked the kind of work I did. That really touched me. I, in turn, thanked them for the fine job they did. They spent thousands of hours putting the case together in meticulous detail.

As we were leaving the courtroom I was dog-tired and noticed the inside of my suit was wet and my shirt was wet clear through. I sweat when I'm in court, even though I'm calm and cool. I saw Holbrock and Bressler in the hallway as we were leaving, and I told Mike to get back up to the third floor and make sure Holbrock and Bressler didn't "backdoor" us with Judge Cramer. "Backdooring" was a term Dick Wessel and I always used to describe a tactic of going in a judge's back door to give some kind of inside information.

When Mike came back, he said it was a damn good thing I sent him upstairs. Holbrock and Bressler were just on their way into Judge Cramer's chambers when they saw him and said, "Oh, Mike, we're glad you're here. We need to talk to the judge." They said they wanted to talk about the fact that the prosecution's case was proceeding so fast (all 101 exhibits were introduced that day). The prosecution was going to be done a day or two ahead of schedule, and the first defense witness wasn't scheduled until Friday, they said.

Mike sat right there with them while they were discussing this with Cramer, and he didn't leave the judge's office until the defense team did. Mike laughed when he relayed this information.

I was sitting with my legs propped up on my desk, not because I was a big-shot, but because my legs hurt all of a sudden. I guess it was some kind of nervous reaction. Mike and I needed to get the testimony lined up from our two General Electric witnesses. It was technical, complicated evidence to build our chain of custody and show how much the Ruppert family had in the estate. Most of the life insurance was through GE.

Mike went home with me, and my oldest boy, John, took him down to the basement to look at my train layout and listen to some steam train records, while I changed clothes. Judy didn't have enough food for both of us, so we went to Johnny Dallis's restaurant, instead. I had some oysters and a Coke, and Mike had a steak. We went back to the office and worked until 2 a.m. Strangely enough, I wasn't tired. I was running on nervous energy and felt really good. We had a good first day, and I was all set for Day 2.

Chapter 22

Most of the trial's second day was taken up with financial testimony, including information about the slain family members' life insurance, assets and holdings. The *Middletown Journal* reported "heated exchanges between the prosecution and defense lawyers."

But the day's most intriguing witness was Ruppert's "Aunt Boots"—Ruby Lee, of Wapakoneta, Ohio, sister of the slain Charity. Lee told the court she had visited Ruppert at jail shortly after his arrest.

"I asked him what happened on that day," Lee testified. "He broke down and cried. He said, 'I don't know,' ... and everything just seemed to be a blank to him."

Lee admitted her family had a long history of mental illness. One of her sisters had suffered from a mental illness, her cousin had died in a mental institution, one of Ruppert's cousins committed suicide, and another attempted suicide, she said.

As she spoke, Ruppert's face reddened and he appeared to be crying.

Lee admitted that she told the prosecution she admonished Ruppert on one occasion. According to her statement, said told the defendant: "You need help and a lot of it."

In spite of this, Lee continued to be a staunch supporter of her nephew throughout the trial. By her own admission, she was perhaps the only supporter who attended on a daily basis.

Chapter 23

John Holcomb

June 17, 1975

It was a beautiful day, not a cloud in the sky. I got up at quarter till seven, just like yesterday. Today my son John got up early, too. His Uncle Tom was going to take him to the farm and transport a truckload of hogs up to the stockyard at Eaton and sell them. There wasn't any breakfast today. Judy was still in bed. So I went down to the office. Dan and Mike were presenting all the evidence and questioning witnesses today.

It was a rough-ass day in court, and it was tough on me, because I didn't do anything but sit there. Dan put all the witnesses on from various banks and insurance companies to testify as to the holdings of Leonard Ruppert and his family, and also James Ruppert. Les Tuttle, the stockbroker, took the witness stand and we didn't get all the evidence out of him that we had expected. Lo and behold, the real bombshell, as far as I was concerned, although nobody commented on it, was when Tuttle said the defense attorneys cashed in about $6,000 worth of stocks for Ruppert on April 8. That knocked my theory into a cocked hat, that Ruppert had maybe $2,500 in stocks and $1,500 in savings. That tore me apart. I came back to the office and Janet ran out to get me a Coke real quick. At least both legs didn't hurt today; only my left leg hurt.

I took Mike home with me for supper again today. We watched the news on television and they showed some artist sketches of the trial. There was a sketch of me shaking my finger in defense attorney Joe Bressler's face. That happened when Dan attempted to get Ruppert's bank deposits into evidence from Wally Mayer, the president of Columbia Federal. The defense objected like hell as to how the police and prosecutor received that information. They were trying to say that Wally gave us the information, which he should not have done, and he did not do. We found the bankbook among Ruppert's possessions.

Even though it was Fischer's witness, I got so damn mad that I jumped out of the chair and went up to the judge's bench and shook my finger right in Bressler's face.

"Just a minute now," I said. "You know that we got the bank book from his house, because I gave you the damn bankbook so you could cash the money in and get a fee."

It just incensed me. In reality, I'd told them all about the bank account and the bankbook so they could get paid. Well, anyway, there was a drawing of that on Channel 2 News, and all my kids were sitting around the TV laughing at me.

Then we had barbecued chicken for supper, and I'll be damned if we didn't eat in the dining room with the tablecloth on the table that night. All the children ate there, too, and they were all little angels. Usually they were throwing their food at each other. I told Mike he really rated, because it was only about the fifth time we'd ever eaten in the dining room. We usually just charged into the kitchen and grabbed a seat at the table.

After supper we sat on the back porch, and Mary Ann and Andy were there. Andy was my little sasser, and he was sassing Mike a little bit. Mary Ann was trying to show off by being a lady, which she never did when I was by myself. Then we pitched baseballs to little Jeff; I was pitching and Mike was catching. Here was my little 3-year-old telling us he batted like Pete Rose. He could actually swing that bat left-handed and hit the ball, too. The only thing was, when he ran to first base, he ran in the wrong direction. It was really cute.

About that time John came home and said Uncle Tom gave him some baby sows. He was going to raise them on the farm that summer and sell them before school started and make some money. I didn't know how that was going to turn out.

We went back to the office, and Mike and I worked our asses off to get ready for Alexander Krysczcak, the payroll man from Schenectady. We called him Kojak. We were trying to get the questions lined up meticulously for this witness. I called Fischer at ten o'clock at night and said, "What's going on?" He just laughed and said he'd come on in. He got there about 10:15. We were on the phone with Krysczcak for about three hours that night. When I got home, Judy told me John wanted to quit the softball team so he could go to the farm every day and raise some pigs to make some money. I told her I thought it was okay with me, but she didn't like the idea. She didn't want him to quit the team.

"Why force the kid to play ball if he doesn't want to play?" I asked her.

We all knew little Jeff was the athlete in the family.

Chapter 24

JOHN HOLCOMB
Wednesday, June 18, 1975

Uncle Tom was supposed to pick up John at seven that morning, but he didn't. Tom always overslept. I told Judy to let John go to the farm. I was anxious to see how the pig business turned out.

Mike spent all morning in court with Krysczcak and took him step by step through every insurance plan, every policy, every benefit that General Electric had, and it was really beautiful. It was a beautiful job the way he took that man, led him right down the path and identified everything. We got all the evidence in. Now we had in evidence something like $220,000 worth of insurance, in addition to all the bank accounts, stocks and bonds.

When we started back this afternoon, I put on Jim Cecere, the real estate agent who appraised the property of Leonard's house on Walter Avenue at $40,000. Leonard also owned rental property appraised at $19,500. And Cecere appraised Charity Ruppert's house at $14,000. Next, we put on Lou Hofstadter, a Hamilton attorney, who testified that in his opinion as an expert in probate law, if Ruppert was found not guilty by reason of insanity, he would inherit all of his brother's estate, all of his mother's estate, and half of the estates of his nieces and nephews.

During the noon hour, we realized that we hadn't really shown that Ruppert had knowledge of his brother's holdings. So I had a brainstorm. I remembered seeing a résumé that Ruppert had prepared for prospective employers, showing that he had also worked at General Electric for several years. My theory was, if I could get that into evidence to show Ruppert worked at GE, he certainly would have had knowledge of GE's benefits for employees.

So I called Dick Carpenter to rush up from the police station. He remembered taking those resumes out of Ruppert's car, along with some tax papers. Well, I put him on the witness stand, and that shows how you rush around on your lunch hour and get yourself all screwed up. I was a mess by the time I got back to court for the afternoon session, but Carpenter's testimony went like clockwork. I got the evidence in.

Also during the trial's third day, Dean Cavett of Greater Cincinnati Coin Center gun shop told the judges that Ruppert broached the subject of obtaining a silencer. The two often ate lunch together during the months prior to his arrest.

"(Ruppert) casually asked where he could get a silencer," Cavett said. "He said, 'With a pillow, you couldn't hear a gun go off.' "

Ruppert also mentioned he had been down near the riverbank firing his .357 rifle on Good Friday and was having trouble hearing him, Cavett said.

The next and final witness was Tuttle. I got him to clarify his testimony from the day before about the stock transaction closed on April 8 by Holbrock and Bressler. Instead of making $6,000, all Ruppert netted out of the transaction was $2,600. He owed Hayden & Stone nearly $4,000, which also came out of that stock transaction. That put me back in the ballgame, as far as my monetary theory went.

As a final witness, I put on Jim Mense, the all-American football player from Hamilton Catholic High School and Notre Dame University. He knew Ruppert way back when. Mense testified that Ruppert called him over to the jail to express concern that his lawyers might be trying to make a deal with the prosecutor. Bressler fell right into my trap and emphasized the fact that Ruppert was afraid his lawyers would make a deal. Then we rested our case.

At that point, Bressler moved for an acquittal under Rule 29 of the Rules of Criminal Procedure. Under Rule 29, the defense was entitled to request a directed verdict at the end of the prosecution's case "if the evidence was insufficient to sustain a conviction."

Bressler argued that the state didn't show Ruppert had knowledge of his brother's assets; didn't show any motive, prior calculation and design; and showed no intent to kill. In fact, he even argued that we didn't prove the defendant did the shooting. When he said that, I just boiled up inside, and when it came my turn to argue, I was really hot. I pointed out that of the 40 bullets fired into those people—and I guess I was probably yelling, I was so worked up—38 of them were lethal. And, of course, you determine the intent to kill from the means used and manner in which it was done. That was elementary. I wasn't worried about that.

Then I went on to argue that prior calculation and design was shown by Ruppert's trying to get a silencer, as well as the fact that the bodies weren't found for three and a half hours (which may give rise to the inference that he did something to silence the gunshots, even though we were unsure what it was). The presence of nitrates on his right hand indicated he fired a gun. The blood on his pants was different from his own type, but the same as some of the children's. There was blood on his shoes, unburned gunpowder with embedded blood on his clothes, which could only have been blown back on him while the bloodbath occurred, and the gun smoke was blowing back and forth in that room. I really laid it on them.

I also argued that brothers have a rough knowledge of what the other is worth. Like I had a rough knowledge of what my brother was worth, and vice versa, even though we really never talked specifically about it. Unfortunately, I said, Leonard Ruppert can't come here to testify about it; he's in the graveyard. And Charity Ruppert can't come here to testify about it: she's in the graveyard. I argued in that vein, then I sat down.

Bressler got up and made a few rebuttal remarks, then the court took it under advisement. Now I knew I had Marrs, but I was worried about Cramer, and didn't know what to think of Fiehrer. I knew how Marrs thought, being a prosecutor for eight years before he became a judge. I knew we were thinking on the same track; I was sure of it. So anyway, I sweated out that 15 minutes that it took them to make up their minds.

When the judges came back, they stated that they unanimously decided there was sufficient evidence for a finding of aggravated murder at this point in the case. The defense motion for a directed verdict, or a reduction in the charge, was overruled. With that, the court recessed until Friday morning.

I was tickled to death that we survived the motion, and it was very clear at that point that it was going to be all or nothing. It was going to be guilty of aggravated murder with a life sentence, or not guilty by reason of insanity. That was what it came down to.

I was glad we had a day of recess coming up, because we had a heck of a lot of work to do. We got back to the office at 2:30 in the afternoon and worked for hours to get our witnesses lined up. Mike was getting the rebuttal witnesses lined up to testify that Ruppert was sane. And while he did that, I was going to get ready to try to handle their psychiatrists. Like my friend Elmer Davidson used to say: I felt like I had as much chance as a one-legged man in an ass-kicking contest. I had to come up with something to handle the defense psychiatrists or dull the edge of what they said, because I knew damn well they were going to say Ruppert was insane. So I had to educate myself in a day and a half—a superhuman feat.

Glenn and Mike went down to Cincinnati to check out some stock records in some of Ruppert's papers. These indicated that he was a big loser prior to the time of the killings. If he took the witness stand, I was going to cross-examine him with those stock records and try to develop them that way. If he denied it, I would bring the witness in from Cincinnati to show in the records that he lost a lot of money in the market. By a lot, I meant he probably invested $4,000 plus another $2,000 that he borrowed on the margin. Then he sold the stocks for $3,000, paid back the $2,000, and he had $1,000 left of his original $4,000. Big loser.

A portrait of the Ruppert family taken shortly before the mass murder. Front row, from left: Thomas, 15; father, Leonard Jr., 42; mother, Alma, 38; John, 4 (on Alma's lap); Teresa, 9; David, 10. Rear, from left: Leonard III, 17; Michael, 16; Carol, 13; Ann, 12. Photo courtesy of findagrave.com.

The Ruppert house at 635 Minor Avenue. Photo by John M. Holcomb.

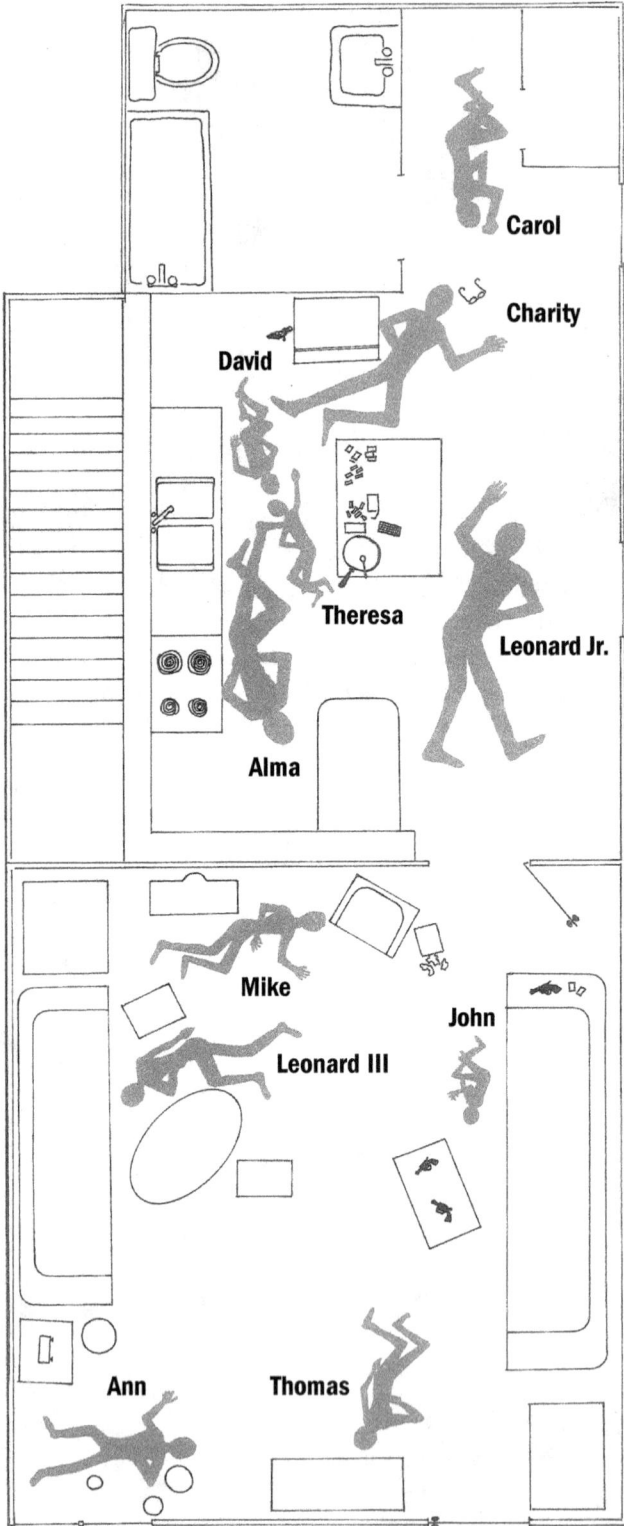

Carol
Charity
David
Theresa
Leonard Jr.
Alma
Mike
John
Leonard III
Ann
Thomas

Diagram courtesy of the Butler County Prosecutor's Office.

The prosecution team in the courtroom, from left: John F. Holcomb, Mike Gmoser, Dan Fischer. Sitting behind the prosecution table, from left: Dan Eichel, intern for the Butler County Prosecutor's Office; spectator Tom Haid, 9; and John M. Holcomb, 9, son of John F. Holcomb. Photo courtesy of the *Hamilton Journal-News*.

Prosecutors Dan Fischer, John F. Holcomb and Mike Gmoser leave the Butler County Courthouse after a day in court. Photo courtesy of the *Hamilton Journal-News*.

James Urban Ruppert sits at the defense table, while defense attorney Hugh Holbrock confers with attorney George Jonson. Photo courtesy of the *Hamilton Journal-News*.

Chapter 25

Jim Irwin described the Ruppert murders as an event that "shook us to the core" and deeply wounded the cities of Hamilton and Fairfield. It was as if residents woke up one day to realize that evil lived in their midst, hidden in a shotgun house on Minor Avenue.

The event changed Vince Isgro's life. Before Easter Sunday 1975, Isgro enjoyed guns and target shooting at a spot across the street from the Great Miami River. Hobbyists regularly set up their own targets there for practice—a pastime Isgro called "plink."

"I went back there and there was a guy there," Isgro said. "He had three guns there. He threw a can out, took a pistol and shot at that can. Every time he shot at that can, the can jumped. Then he switched to a rifle when the can got too far away. The guy was very cold. There was no conversation."

The "guy" was James Ruppert. Soon after, Vince saw him at the 19th Hole and sat near him at the bar. Ruppert nodded in his direction, as if he recognized him, but declined to speak. After the murders, Vince told his story to Holcomb and police officer Dick Holzberger during dinner at a local restaurant called Waldo's Supper Club.

"It was two to three days after the killing," Isgro said. "I saw his picture and told them I knew him. Next thing I knew, I was subpoenaed."

He was 29 and terrified.

"It really put me on edge," Isgro said. "Things that went through my mind were protecting my family. I thought he'd come after me. It just gives me the jeebies when I think I was alone with him and he had a gun. I was a gun guy. I had guns and target shot. After this happened—that was it with the guns."

Isgro eventually moved his family to California for a work opportunity and ended up staying there for many years before moving back to Hamilton. Almost every Easter Sunday since 1975, locals have posted their memories of the Ruppert murders on social media.

"I'd like to put that behind me," Isgro said, "and it just keeps coming back to haunt me."

On the 25th anniversary of the murders, defense attorney Bressler echoed Isgro's sentiment.

"In all honesty, I really don't want to relive the case," he told *Journal-News* Managing Editor Dirk Allen in a rare interview in 2000. "I've worked very hard to put it behind me. It was a horrible tragedy then, and it's still a horrible tragedy 25 years later. I don't feel there's any benefit to bringing it up now."

The only glimpse Bressler gave into that night was that he had had "kind of a different feeling" about the phone call he received from Ruppert on March 30, 1975. He had changed from his "old knock-about clothes," shaved, and went to meet Ruppert with his law partner Holbrock.

"When I got to the City Building, the whole front of it was lit up by media coverage people... For the first time, I understood the totality of what was involved."

"It's the kind of case, once you're involved in it you never forget it," Bressler said. "It gave me a lot of trial experience—hopefully it helped me as an attorney and a judge... But it was an experience that I would have gladly forgone."

Decades later, he would still experience occasional "flashes of horror" triggered by viewing the photographs of the children.

Chuck Mignery understands that feeling all too well. As a student who rode the school bus with Lenny and a pallbearer who carried Lenny and Ann's caskets at the funeral, he was deeply affected by the murders. He remembers the long, somber procession to the cemetery.

"Imagine eleven hearses. Eleven," he said.

Mignery has visited the cemetery a few times over the decades. "It's a very humbling experience to go there today and see plot after plot after plot... Ruppert, Ruppert, Ruppert...."

The longtime world history teacher at Badin High School still tells his students about the murders and his connection to them. About 25 years ago, a group of Badin journalism students made a documentary about the killings and asked Mignery to critique it. He watched it late one night in his basement after his family had gone to bed, and was stunned to see that the students had included gruesome crime-scene photos of the bodies lying in pools of blood.

"I started crying, right there alone in my basement," he said.

Whenever he showed the documentary, he covered the crime-scene photos and told people they should remember the children as they were at school, vibrant and alive. He remembers Lenny was "strong as an ox" and won every handshake contest he entered. Mike was the goofy prankster nicknamed "Possum."

Mignery's only regret is not writing a letter to James Ruppert asking him why he snuffed out all those lives. He attended the trial a few times and will never forget the reaction when the mass murderer entered the courtroom.

"Ruppert walked in, and you could feel the hush," he said. "He just sat there."

Chapter 26

JOHN HOLCOMB
Thursday, June 19, 1975

The trial was in recess for a day, so I ran through a quickie divorce, the proceeds of which would tide me over for a couple more weeks. Then I started my preparation for the cross-examination of the psychiatrists, which was really a bitch of a task because I was trying to learn a lot of psychiatry in one day's time. I'd gone through a lot of my old files and records from past cases, which were going to help me a lot.

We got a bombshell that really caused my skin to tingle. We received information from Martha "Bea" Carr, a good friend of Ruppert and one of the witnesses whom Ebbing went out to interview last night to double-check her statement. Ruppert had been writing to her and she had been writing to him in jail. Martha was a good friend of Charity, also.

On May 9, 1975, Ruppert wrote:

Dear Bea:

I very much appreciate your concern for me. I regret that you won't be able to visit me, because I'm allowed only three names on my visitor's list and list is filled. I would like to see you, though. No, there isn't anything I need. Thanks for asking. I often think of you and Bob and wonder if Mike has found his direction yet. It's unfortunate that he spent so much time in training, then didn't actually use it. But he's still very young and has many opportunities to accomplish some other career. Where are you working now? Say hi to Bob for me. I'll close for now.

Yours Truly,

Jim

The next one was dated May 23, 1975:

Dear Bea and Bob,

Glad to hear that you're working at the (Ohio) Casualty, and the nice thing about being in the old A&P Building is that you don't have to walk up and down stairs, for whatever that's worth. I know you get enough exercise! What are they going to do in that area where they tore down the Mack building, etc.? Bea, I know what you mean about that graduation picture. I just saw one myself the other day. I had forgot that I had different front teeth at that time. I graduated in '52 with 48 in the class. How is it that there were only three in your class? What kind of trouble is Bob having that he can't walk too well? Do the two of you travel much these days on holiday weekends, etc.? I was thinking that Bob has a part-time job somewhere, has he? I haven't seen Ski for so long, how is he and what's he doing these days? Last I knew, he had patented some new invention. How's that going? What's new with Mike? Well, that's enough questions for a while. I'll close for now. God bless and keep you.

Love,

Jim

The next letter came on May 31, 1975:

Dear Bea,

Just a note to ask you to please bring me the items listed on the enclosed card. You can bring these items any hour of the day and leave them at the control room, the window marked information just inside the front door here at 123 Court Street. Just tell the deputy at that window to give them to me right away. Tell him that I said for him to pay you out of the money in my property. You can probably get most all those things at Ontario's and the barbershop in the Plaza Shopping Center. Matches at Super-Value store near the Ontario store. How are things at your house these days? Bea, do you work Saturdays or just Monday through Friday? How did you happen to get a job at Casualty? I'll close for now.

  Gratefully,

  Jim

The card read:

> 2 boxes of pad matches—50 pads per box
>
> 1 pair of sponge rubber insoles—men's size 8
>
> 1 container of Mennen shave talc
>
> 1 scalp massager—they coast about 75 cents and can be bought at barbershops and other places—they are plastic about three inches in diameter and have many prongs on the underside that massage the scalp

We planned to call Bea as a rebuttal witness. She didn't believe Ruppert committed the murders and thought he was normal and sane, which of course, appeared evident from the letters. Those weren't the work of a crazy man. The bombshell is that Bea told us that the start of the next week after the murders, she went to the Goody Shop, which is owned and operated by Gus and Edna Skalkos, an elderly Greek couple who had been in business in Hamilton for a long time. I used to go to their place when it was on High Street 30 years ago, when I was 8 years old. I would get a bowl of chili or a coney island for a dime.

Bea worked at Ohio Casualty right next to this restaurant and ate lunch there every day. She knew Mrs. Skalkos really well and told her she was a really good friend of the Ruppert family. Mrs. Skalkos told her, "Why, those boys were in here Saturday morning (the day before the murders)!" By "boys," she was referring to brothers Leonard and Jim Ruppert. Mrs. Skalkos said she saw the taller brother, Leonard, order breakfast, take some back to Jim in a booth, and sit down to eat with him. During the time they were eating, the taller one, Leonard, kept making motions with his hands like he was bawling Jim out, like he was giving Jim hell about something, although they were talking low and she couldn't hear what he was saying. That was my bombshell. That was the one I was going to drop in their lap.

What happened, sure as hell, was that Jim was in financial trouble with his stock market transactions and went to his brother for another loan. His brother was giving him hell, probably saying, "Why don't you save your money and put it in the bank instead of blowing it in the stock market?" I was elated to hear that from Bea earlier today, but it had worn off a little.

Mrs. Skalkos said she was not going to testify in court. I told her that was OK; we just wanted to know what she knew. She really didn't know she was going to be a witness, but what the hell, I can't worry about whether she wants to come to court or not. That's one of her duties as a citizen. I know she won't care once she gets up there, because she and her husband are good people.

· · · · ·

All afternoon and evening, I worked on the cross-examination of Dr. Lester Grinspoon. My friend Jim Irwin (I really owed him a debt of gratitude) researched and photocopied every article Dr. Grinspoon had ever written. Grinspoon was a hotshot from Harvard who had written 50-some articles and a couple of books and was one of the best psychiatrists in the country. I was scared to death. There was no way I could handle him, so I was just going to spar with him a little bit and let him think I was just a country dummy. In one of these articles, Grinspoon wrote, "The inability of trained judges to agree on the diagnostic classification of psychiatric patients has been repeatedly demonstrated. This disagreement increases as the function of the fineness of the differentiation attempted and the number of judges involved." Then Grinspoon went on to write: "Thus, a given diagnosis conveys minimal information concerning the individuals so classified and empirical studies based on such designations are correspondingly difficult to evaluate."

So you see, I had something there that I could use to my advantage, if I got a break and could play the country dummy for about

15 minutes with him. I was going to ask, "It's true, isn't it, that the inability of trained psychiatrists to agree on the diagnostic classification of psychiatric patients has been repeatedly demonstrated?" If he said yes, good. If he said no, I had him. Then I would ask, "It's true, isn't it, that the disagreement increases with the fineness of the differentiation attempted and the number of psychiatrists involved?" Regardless of what his answer was, I had him. Then I'd ask, "Isn't it true that a given diagnosis conveys little information concerning the individual so classified?" And regardless of his answer, I had him. So I was praying that this held together and I could spring that trap. That way, the man from Boston would have flown in and flown back out for nothing. God, I hoped it would hold together.

Dan and Mike and I took an hour out in the evening and went to the One High Club and each got a steak. Dan and Mike both forgot their money, so I got stuck with the tab for $30.87. But I paid it happily, plus a $5 tip, because I was so tickled to death. It had been a beautiful day.

At 10:00 that night I still had to get ready for all the other doctors and psychologists, because I didn't know in what order they would be called. I'd be working till three or four o'clock in the morning. But I couldn't wait to get back in the courtroom. I was chomping at the bit now that I had something to look forward to. If I could just hang in there one more day, I was going to take my chances.

Chapter 27

The defense, of course, presented an opposing view of Ruppert during its case. Bressler and Holbrook conceded that Ruppert had indeed committed the murders, but argued that he was legally insane and unable to refrain from his actions.

Nine private psychiatrists, two court-appointed psychiatrists and four psychologists examined Ruppert after his arrest, and all concluded he was mentally and legally insane. His mental illness dated back to his youth, when he lived in a one-room makeshift house in a "chicken coop," Bressler said in his opening statement on Friday, June 20, 1975.

"The psychosis developed, developed and developed until March 30, 1975," Bressler argued. "All the problems exploded" and Ruppert "caused the death of the family and children that were so dear to him."

The first defense witness, the eminent Dr. Grinspoon from Harvard Medical School, diagnosed Ruppert as paranoid, which he described as "a psychosis which severely limits one's capacity to recognize and deal with reality." Ruppert believed he was the victim of a conspiracy to paint him as a homosexual and a communist and was convinced that his brother had been systematically sabotaging his car and preventing him from obtaining employment.

On the day of the murders, Leonard's "How's your Volkswagen?" remark and "big mocking smile" incited an overwhelming rage to explode inside Ruppert. That rage rendered him unable to refrain from the murders, Grinspoon said.

Ruppert had told Grinspoon he had been to the 19th Hole bar the night before Easter Sunday, got home around two-thirty in the morning, and slept until four o'clock in the afternoon. At that point, he went downstairs and visited with his family, watched the children hunt Easter eggs, chatted with Leonard about the stock market, and told everyone he was going target-shooting, as he did every Sunday afternoon.

Ruppert then went upstairs to his bedroom to retrieve his three pistols and one rifle, all of which he kept loaded in case of prowlers, the psychiatrist testified. Ruppert was passing through the kitchen with his loaded guns when he heard the fateful question.

"How's your Volkswagen?" Leonard asked, displaying what the psychiatrist characterized as a mocking grin.

Ruppert shot his brother in the chest, causing him to fall back in a chair. "Call the police," Leonard instructed his family members.

But it was too late. Ruppert continued firing until everyone was dead.

"His ego was just completely overwhelmed by this rage, this suppressed rage he had been accumulating over some ten years or more—actually since childhood," Grinspoon testified. "And there was no way in which he could avoid doing that act."

After the shootings, Ruppert lay on the sofa for three hours contemplating suicide. He decided against taking his own life, because it was considered a mortal sin in Catholic doctrine. Instead, he went upstairs and changed his clothing, which he considered "too effeminate," and called police.

Ruppert told Grinspoon he was a sickly child who suffered from asthma, prohibiting him from participating in many childhood activities. His father died of tuberculosis when he was a boy, and he felt his brother and mother had always been against him. His mother wanted a daughter, and often told Ruppert he should have been a girl. She tried to feminize him by styling his hair and communicating to him in "baby talk." Ruppert also told Grinspoon his mother hated him, beat him, and taunted him. She encouraged Leonard to take part in the punishments. When Ruppert was about 15, his mother and brother took him to the basement and beat him with a rubber hose as punishment for throwing a dinner plate to the floor. He later considered suicide, and even tied a sheet around his neck and secured it to the bed post, planning to jump out the window. But he "lost his courage," he told the psychiatrist.

He was hospitalized with spinal meningitis at age 18. Ruppert started seeing a psychologist in 1960, when he was having trouble with his college work. He visited other mental health professionals in later years.

At age 26, Ruppert discovered he was impotent and blamed his mother, Grinspoon reported.

"That destroyed me," Ruppert told Grinspoon. "My mother succeeded. I was no longer a man."

His overwhelming preoccupation of the last 10 years was the "conspiracy" headed by his mother, brother and the FBI, Grinspoon testified. The feeling continued to haunt him over a decade.

"He feels his jail cell is bugged and distrusts his attorneys," the doctor said.

The *Middletown Journal* called Grinspoon's testimony "the most dramatic moment of the trial so far." Courtroom spectators were spellbound, and Ruppert appeared to cry when the doctor was on the stand.

During Grinspoon's testimony, the 60 courtroom seats were filled, and about 20 additional spectators lined the courtroom walls. Others waited in the corridor to catch a glimpse of Ruppert coming and going in handcuffs. Judge Cramer said it reminded him of the spectacle surrounding the trials of Marie Abbott and her young farmhand lover, Scotty Gordon, who were tried and convicted of murdering Marie's wealthy husband, Morris, in 1948. They had placed his body on the railroad tracks to make the murder look like an accidental death. During that sensational case, observers packed the same courtroom, vehicular traffic came to a standstill outside, and spectators lined the streets to catch a glimpse of the defendants. Presiding at the Abbott trials was Judge Cramer, who now was at the helm of arguably the most infamous case ever heard inside the walls of the 19th century Butler County Courthouse.

Chapter 28

All six psychiatrists and two psychologists who testified as expert defense witnesses claimed Ruppert had a major mental illness that rendered him unable to distinguish between right and wrong or resist the split-second impulse to gun down his entire family. The defense doctors testified that Ruppert acted in a fit of uncontrollable rage. They also agreed that his mental illness was too ingrained and complex for him to fake.

Dr. Phillip Mechanick, a professor of psychiatry at the University of Pennsylvania, testified that Ruppert "reflexly" gunned down his family members without realizing what he was doing.

"At the point his brother asked him about his car, then his internal perception of himself altered abruptly and dramatically," Mechanick said. "At that point, he described to me a whole rush of thoughts, memories, and fantasies about what his brother had done to him, both in terms of damage to his vehicle and other injurious acts."

Ruppert lived in an alternate reality, in which he misinterpreted events to confirm his suspicions of a conspiracy, the psychiatrist said.

He did not think about his actions, until he heard "the moaning and groaning of the children," and thought he "should put them out of their misery," Mechanick said.

His equating the children to injured animals that needed to be euthanized showed he had no comprehension of right and wrong, Mechanick said.

Judge Cramer asked Dr. Mechanick how Ruppert would have reacted to his brother's comment had he not been carrying loaded guns at that moment.

"The defendant would not have acted at that point," Mechanick answered.

He described it as a perfect storm of events and opportunity.

"Impulse was there, rage was there, and the remedy means were there," he said.

Mechanick added that "even a well-trained psychiatrist" could not fake the illness that afflicted Ruppert.

Dr. Glenn Weaver, a psychiatrist who treated Ruppert between 1961 and 1965, said he was shocked at the deterioration he saw in the defendant's condition when he visited him in his jail cell.

"He immediately burst into tears and just uncontrollable weeping," Weaver said. "His eyes were glassy. There was an absence of facial expression, despite his tears. It was appalling."

When he began treating Ruppert in 1961, he was "an unhappy man" who considered himself as a loser and suffered from a type of masochism.

"I can never win," Ruppert had told him. "I can't even kill myself."

His mental illness began to develop after a librarian made a snide comment about his boring life. That triggered him to make an obscene phone call to the Lane Library, which led to a subsequent police investigation. At the time, Weaver encouraged Ruppert to move out of his mother's house and try to salvage his life. In a letter referring Ruppert to a psychiatrist in Columbus, Weaver wrote that Charity "at times, crossed the line" into psychosis.

Ruppert's paranoia grew out of his earlier masochistic tendencies, Weaver believed. He said the defendant suffered from delusions that his mother, brother, the FBI, the CIA and others were out to get him. On the day of the murders, his brother's innocent remark about the VW catapulted Ruppert into a rage, according to Weaver.

He "went berserk," Weaver said.

Back in 1961, Ruppert reported to Dr. Weaver that he had a bizarre and vivid dream that he was facing a death sentence in a courtroom similar to Judge Cramer's. Weaver showed the court Ruppert's sketch and three-page handwritten account of the dream, which eerily foreshadowed the defendant's current circumstances. The psychiatrist interpreted the dream as a sign of the guilt Ruppert felt back then.

The Dream
As Written By James Ruppert
November 1, 1961

In my dream, I was seated at a long table (about 15 feet). I had been condemned to death (for no known reason) and my friends were gathered around me. The table was covered with white cloth or white paper and was some 10 feet from the wall.

During the dream, there was no mention of the way I would be put to death but each time I would think of it (in dream) I pictured myself being electrocuted, and in the dream this thought came to me some 3 or 4 times. Each time it came to me, I was happy at the thought that the end (destiny of either heaven or hell) was so close; I kept thinking "this is it" what I've waited for all my life.

And yet, I was still somewhat afraid—not at the thought of hell, but at the uncertainty of what really does happen after death. Then, at this point I would tell myself that it really doesn't make too much difference (I was still convinced of "eternity") and that whatever was to come next, even if it were to be unhappy for me, was for eternity and that compared to that, even my entire life span (which is partly spent already) is infinitesimal. And no consideration that it would be foolish to be in agony because death was coming since life itself (in time) is nothing to speak of.

But people about me mourned and eventually there were tears in the eyes of the nearest ones (distance & feeling). The person next to me spoke, and in talking to me, found out that I didn't believe something of the type that "conscientious objectors" believe and are permitted to serve their time (sentence) in some other form/way.

Someone near him picked up on that idea and loudly began to appeal to the court. When I heard this I strongly & loudly pleaded with him not to pursue his appeal. The conviction I had that he was using to save my life was, when (in dream) I gave it a second's thought, ridiculous to use since the believing of it really had no bearing on duty or justice (like not believing in capital punishment should keep a man from being put to death).

When I had quieted him, the crowd had begun to mumble and moan because I was washing away all hope of saving my life and the (same) fellow next to me was crying and pleading with me to cling to this last straw—and as all this was happening, I was aware that I had just less than two minutes to live or in which to save or prolong my life. The crowd was louder and louder and more crying and sympathy and moaning had caused me to be sad, and yet I was still happy but was giving way to this mass mood and in all (indecipherable) I was still begging the man next to me, who I now recognized as a man who looked much like my dad, and at the last crying very hard and still begging him & everyone else not to make it any harder for me.

By this time I was almost as hysterical as the crowd and was still troubled by a shred of uncertainty about what comes after death, but some 90 percent of me was still fighting for the climax merely on faith & the reasoning of a few years versus eternity.

At the last, I was still begging the fellow, "Please don't make this more difficult for me, Jerry." At that point I awoke and was very happy (at the first instant) that I was only dreaming. Then I immediately fell into a very deep sadness and cried loud and very hard, begging God's forgiveness for all that I've done wrong, and feeling happy that I wasn't really dying in sin.

Although in the dream (which, in the dream, lasted for about 10 min.), I never gave any concern to the idea of whether or not I was in sin and made no attempt to ask for forgiveness.

Other defense witnesses testified that Ruppert suffered from major mental illness. Dr. D.C. Stevens, a Hamilton psychiatrist, testified that the paranoid Ruppert clung to the delusion of a widespread conspiracy against him. He even suspected that a local newspaper reporter covering the trial was an FBI agent in disguise. While Ruppert recalled all of the incidents leading up to the shooting, the violence itself was "all in a daze," the psychiatrist told the court.

Dr. Leigh M. Roberts, a professor of psychiatry at the University of Wisconsin, testified that Ruppert concealed his emotions from others, because he feared they might be involved in the conspiracy. Roberts's diagnosis of Ruppert was similar to the other mental health professionals who testified for the defense.

During four hours on the stand, Roberts outlined Ruppert's life history and the events that led to the mass shooting. He used a blackboard to detail different types of paranoid behavior and the terminology to describe each one. All are considered psychosis, a major mental illness, he said. A diagnosis of "paranoid personality" is an exception, Roberts said.

Dr. Henry Bachrach, also of the University of Pennsylvania, testified that Ruppert was an "extremely fearful, suspicious and passive person" whose thoughts were "permeated with violence" and "angry, sadistic feelings" about women. He agreed that Ruppert had been mentally ill for many years.

Ruppert's IQ of 118 to 120 placed him in the top 20 percent of the population, he said.

"He's a very bright man, but his thinking is twisted," Bachrach added.

Dr. Lester Grinspoon testified that Ruppert's shyness concealed his mental illness from those around him.

"You rarely find these people in hospitals, because they can get on so well in the community," Grinspoon testified. "The hallmark of his illness is confined to just part of his ego. Very few people knew about it ... He didn't reveal it, and there was nothing bizarre about his personality."

Chapter 29

JOHN HOLCOMB
Friday, June 20, 1975

Dr. Grinspoon of Harvard University was the opening defense witness. They were firing their big gun first. I had nerves—the pre-game jitters again. It was because of this Grinspoon fellow. There was no way I could match wits with him. If I could just get the first paragraph of his article into evidence, I'd be satisfied.

So they brought Dr. Grinspoon in and he took the witness stand. It took about 20 or 30 minutes for him to recite all of his qualifications. During the course of that, he stated that he had written three books, and two of them had been translated and published in foreign countries, and he had written 81 articles—81 of them—and he went through all of his many other qualifications. He was an eminent psychiatrist, of that there was no question.

Fischer and Gmoser were writing like the devil, writing down every word that he said, and I just sat there, unconcerned, looking around the courtroom. I was just trying to act real cool. He went on and on, and I was very impressed with the man. His conclusion, he said, was that Ruppert was suffering from a rare form of psychotic paranoia and had a fixed delusional system, or fixed false beliefs. Grinspoon impressed me as a nice guy and a gentleman, until the tail-end of questioning. For the last question, Bressler asked Grinspoon what he thought about the prosecution's contention that Ruppert was faking insanity and committed the murders to gain an inheritance.

"That is only slightly less impressive an illusion than the delusions of a conspiracy by the defendant," Grinspoon replied.

That made me so goddamned mad I couldn't see straight, so I thought I'd just get right down to the brass tacks with that Ivy League pompous SOB. I thought he was nice before he pulled that Ivy League bullshit on me and ended up being a smart-aleck bastard. Pardon my language.

"Doctor," I said, "will you repeat the last answer so I get it absolutely right?"

"Well, I'm not sure I remember it exactly," Grinspoon replied.

"Well, let me help you," I said. "You said that is only slightly less impressive an illusion..."

"Let me think a second," he said. "That is only slightly less impressive an illusion than the delusions of the defendant."

I was on the right track with him in my own mind.

"I don't mean to be offensive, Doctor, but state the exact terms of your employment with the defendant," I said.

Hugh Holbrock jumped up and objected. Cramer overruled the objection.

"I get $600 a day plus expenses," Grinspoon said.

"What are the total charges to date?" I asked.

He told me they were $1,200 and his expenses were $150 to $200. I asked when he first saw the defendant, and he answered it was May 8 or 9 for four or five hours.

"Of course, I saw him again last night," he added.

I didn't go into that, but I knew he only stopped in the jail the previous night for 15 minutes. I asked about the history that Ruppert gave him, specifically with regard to homosexuality. Grinspoon said the defendant reported having one homosexual experience. And then I asked him if he had given him any history about what he did the day before Easter. He said Ruppert had told him he was in a bar drinking that night.

"What did he tell you about the daytime?" I asked.

He said nothing.

"Did you ask him?" I questioned.

"No," Grinspoon replied.

Then I asked him about the target shooting, and he said the defendant mentioned that was his hobby.

"Isn't it true," I asked, "that one psychiatric dictionary called Hinsie & Campbell lists 66 different types of insanity?"

"That is true," he said.

"How long after the killing was your examination?" I asked.

He allowed that it was some five weeks or so after the murders.

"Doctor, isn't it naturally difficult to make retrospective statements about a person's state of mind at a given time in the past?" I asked. "Isn't this true?"

The doctor answered no, that he didn't think that was true. Then I asked if he interviewed any of the defendant's relatives, coworkers, neighbors, or acquaintances, and he said no. It's Standard Operating Procedure, or SOP, as he phrased it, not to do any of that and make judgment strictly on what the guy tells him.

"Well in that case, your only source of information was the defendant himself?" I asked.

He said that wasn't strictly true, because he had received a report from Dr. Mechanick and the psychologists, along with other information.

"Doctor, did the defendant realize the purpose of your examination, and that you might be called into court to testify as to his mental condition?" I asked.

"Yes."

"Might a man who faces the death penalty exaggerate the symptoms of abnormality during a psychiatric examination?" I asked.

"Yes."

"Doctor, are you of the belief that a person's every act is determined by forces over which he has no control?" I asked.

"No, I'm not," he said.

"Would it be your belief, then, that a person does exercise some free will?" I asked.

"Yes," the doctor said. "However, let me qualify that: not when a man is as sick as this defendant."

103

He probably thought I was going to argue a little bit of psychiatry with him then, and he was going to beat my brains out, but I didn't do that. I cited the quote from the article he'd written, the one I'd been waiting to use.

I asked, "It's true, isn't it, Doctor, that the inability of trained psychiatrists to agree on diagnostic classifications has been shown time and time again?"

"Yes, to a certain extent," Grinspoon answered.

"Isn't it true that this disagreement increases with the fineness of the differentiation attempted and the number of psychiatrists involved?" I asked.

He said no, not necessarily.

"Doctor, isn't that exactly the reason that a given diagnosis conveys little if any information concerning the individual so classified?" I asked.

"No," he said. "Absolutely not."

Well, my trap sprang shut—right on his leg.

I took my time and I walked over to the counsel table, even though I was so excited I could hardly stand it. I opened my briefcase and, one by one, I flopped out a stack of 20 to 25 of the articles Grinspoon had written. Naturally, I had it planned that the one I wanted was on the bottom. All this took a couple of minutes. When I got the one I wanted, I was leaning across the table looking at Mike Gmoser, and I said in a voice loud enough for the people in the first row to hear: "Now I'm going to shove his illusion up his ass."

I turned around and went back to the podium.

"Doctor," I said. "Of the 81 articles you have written, I'll direct your attention to one you wrote in June 1965, which appeared in Volume 27 of the *Journal of Psychosomatic Medicine*. Do you remember that?"

He said he did.

"Doctor, I'm going to read the first paragraph of that article to you," I said.

And I read the first paragraph in the last three questions I asked him, the most significant one being the very last sentence that diagnostic classification doesn't mean anything.

"Now I'm going to let you read it, so you know what I'm talking about," I told the psychiatrist.

He read it, and I asked, "Now, did you write that paragraph?"

"No, I didn't actually write that paragraph," he said. "But I coauthored the article, so I guess I have to take responsibility for it. However..."

He seemed so confused and rattled that he read the paragraph out loud, real fast, just Ratta-tat-tat, and by the time he got to the end of it, he had an answer for me, because he was "courtroom wise," a real sharp dude.

He went on to explain for two or three minutes that the paragraph and that article didn't have any relevance to what we were talking about. And I just turned my back to him and stood there and shook my head. When he finished, I walked back up to him.

"Thank you very much, Doctor," I told him. "Have a pleasant trip back."

I felt like a million bucks. When I was springing my trap, I could tell Judge Cramer knew something was coming, because he was peering out over the top of his glasses at me. I loved that the guy was so sharp, he knew me so well, and knew my style so well, that he knew something was coming. The other two judges didn't know what was coming, but when I sat down, Judges Marrs and Fiehrer had big smiles on their faces. Cramer didn't, but Marrs and Fiehrer did.

At noon recess, Dick Wessel approached me in the hallway and grabbed my hand.

"John, I just want to tell you that was the most masterful cross-examination that I've ever seen," he said.

I was so touched I almost cried. Dick Wessel was a real bulldog of a cross-examiner with good style and technique. After trying all the big cases with him for eight years when he was prosecutor, I watched him do all the heavy work on the cross-examinations and expert witnesses and thought he was great. My role in those cases was to play the razzle-dazzle man in the final argument. Wessel would be the straight man and get up and outline the facts and proof, and then the defense would give its argument, then I'd get up and give them quotations, bring on the histrionics, and make them cry and yell and shout. That's why Dick's compliment really touched me. He went back to the office with Mike, Glenn, and me, and we drank a coke and relaxed and talked. I felt like a million bucks.

· · · · · ·

When we went back into the courtroom after recess, I told Mike this was too damn good to last. And it was. The defense put on Dr. Howard Sokolov from the Forensic Center, a psychiatrist from Cincinnati. Sokolov testified that Ruppert was, in his opinion, psychotic and suffering from a "paranoid state." He knew the difference between right and wrong, but could not resist doing the wrong; he had an irresistible impulse. The only concession I got from Sokolov was that he assumed all the information Ruppert gave him was true.

"Doctor, what if I can show that Ruppert went upstairs for the purpose of getting guns to kill the family?" I asked. "Would your answer be the same?"

He replied that he could not give an answer under those circumstances. I sat down on that note, because it left the door open for me to prove that Ruppert did in fact have knowledge that he was going to kill his family beforehand. That knowledge, I planned to argue, nullified Sokolov's opinion.

Mary Veleta Sears took the stand next. She ate at Frisch's Restaurant with five or six others, including Ruppert, almost every day. On one occasion, she said something to him, and he replied, "Ssshhh... Castro's talking to me." That was the end of the defense's examination of Mary.

I got up and asked, "Well, you didn't think he was crazy at the time, did you?"

"No," she answered. "I thought he had ESP."

That answer, in my view, made Mary seem crazy herself.

Court adjourned for the day, and Mike and I went back to the office. We always reviewed our notes from the day and tried to stress good and bad points from the proceedings. Mike's wife, Olga, was waiting in the office for us, as was Fran, my secretary. Fran was off for the summer, but she had been watching the trial for a couple of days. Olga and Fran were longtime friends and decided to go shopping or something, since Mike and I had to work late. But the two women called us later from the One High Club and asked us to join them for dinner. We had a nice dinner together, laughing and telling jokes, and then the waitress presented me with the tab for $43.89. I knew Mike was just starting out, so I insisted on paying. I was glad to do it, because I was so damn happy about the way things went in court that day. Mike, Olga and Fran all went home, but I walked back up High Street to the office. It started to rain, but it felt so good. It was a thunderstorm, even, but I took my time and walked on up the street in the pouring rain. Back at the office, I just sat there until about 11:00. I had plans to meet Glenn over at Waldo's, so I drove over there and started talking about the case with him.

When Glenn Ebbing and Charlie Reid were partners on the detective squad, we solved some of our best cases over a little Hudepohl beer at night. It struck me over the course of the years that these guys would come up with some really good ideas when they got out and drank a little beer, but the next day neither they nor I could remember what the ideas were. We didn't sit around getting drunk, mind you, but just had a few beers. So I made it a practice to jot little notes on the bar napkin during our conversations. One idea I jotted down that night was that Ruppert claimed the only reason he didn't kill himself the night of the murders was because he believed suicide was a mortal sin. In rebuttal, we'd put on Francis Pierson, who said Ruppert told him he didn't believe in God.

After a couple more beers, I had an absolutely brilliant brainstorm. The defense made a suggestion in its case as to Charity Ruppert's character. They claimed part of the reason for Ruppert's mental condition was that his mother forced him to sleep in bed with her one night when he was 15 or 16, and he woke to find her unclothed and his hand had been placed in a compromising position. He knew he didn't put it there. That was a scurrilous suggestion. Ruppert also suggested his brother was cruel and sadistic to him. So my brainstorm was to get the parish priest at St. Ann's Church to testify that Charity was a good person of high moral character. That would help us with Judge Fiehrer, because he lived in that neighborhood and attended that church. And the other half of the brainstorm was to get the parish priest at Sacred Heart—Leonard's church—to testify that Leonard wasn't cruel or sadistic, but a nice guy.

Glenn suggested we put on Johnny Wynn, an older fellow who used to date Charity many years ago, and Bea Carr, the family friend who was writing to Ruppert in jail, to say Charity had the highest morals. I wrote that on my napkin, folded it up and tucked it in my pocket. Glenn leaned toward me and said a guy at the bar was trying to make trouble by "wising off" to him.

"I've never seen him before," Glenn said, "but I tell you he's going to come over here, and when he does, I'm going to kick his ass."

"Oh, no, pal," I said. "That's all we need: to get into a damn barroom fight right in the middle of this trial, or any time, as far as that goes. I can see the headlines now: 'Prosecutor and detective in barroom brawl.' I'll be going to court Monday, have a black eye or teeth kicked out. Look. We don't need this—not anytime, but especially not now."

"Well, I guess you're right on that," Glenn agreed.

I swallowed my drink in one gulp. Glenn still had a full bottle of beer. When the man in question got up to use the restroom, I grabbed Glenn.

"Let's get the hell out of here," I said.

So we ducked out the back door and drove back to our respective homes.

It reminded me of a time back in 1967, when a guy got shot in a local bar down on skid row. Glenn and I were called in on the investigation. I was at the police station, and Hugh Holbrock came running in all out of breath. He was wearing his cowboy suit that he always wore. He said somebody stole his hat. He asked Glenn to go get it for him. Glenn said if Holbrook filled out a stolen property report, he would go get it. He was just jacking him around, but Hugh filled out the report. Glenn went down to this place called Gracie's Bar, down on Vine Street. Apparently, after the shooting, the defendant called Hugh to represent him, and Hugh went charging down to the joint. It was a tough place and he told everyone there he was a lawyer for the defendant and wanted to get witness statements from all of them. There was one old guy sitting at the bar with both elbows and a glass of beer in front of him, staring into his beer and taking a sip once in a while. Hugh went up to him, introduced himself, and said he wanted to get a statement from him.

"I'm sitting here drinking my beer minding my own business, and I don't want to be bothered by you," the man said. "So why don't you just move along?"

Hugh argued that, as the defendant's lawyer, he had a right to get a statement from him.

"I'm just sitting here drinking my beer and don't want to be bothered with you," the man repeated. "The next time you bother me, I'm going to knock you on your ass."

So the man turned around and started drinking his beer again.

"That would be the biggest mistake you ever made," Hugh told him. "I was the middleweight champion of the Pacific Fleet."

With that, the man jumped up from the bar, hit Hugh in the jaw, and knocked off his cowboy hat. Hugh jumped up, ran out the door, and ran for six blocks to the police station. So Glenn went down and got his hat and brought it back to him. Hugh reached out to take his hat.

"Uh-uh," Glenn said. "You have to sign a receipt for it first—a return property receipt."

So Hugh filled it out, and Glenn gave him his hat back. That was going back a long time.

It was one o'clock when I got home, and everyone was in bed. I went upstairs and climbed into my own bed, exhausted.

Chapter 30

JOHN HOLCOMB
Saturday, June 21, 1975

I woke up and got *The Cincinnati Post* and the *Hamilton Journal-News* from the doorstep. I couldn't wait to see what they wrote about my brilliant cross-examination of Grinspoon. Both papers published everything that Grinspoon said, but not a single word about my cross-examination. It went right over the public's head, I guessed, but I didn't care. All I cared about was that it didn't go over the judges' heads.

I decided to walk to work, because I hadn't been getting much exercise lately. Not that I ever got that much, but the thing I noticed since I was putting in long hours was I was smoking about four packs of cigarettes a day. I usually smoked two, but I was up to four packs and had a terrible cough. So I figured if I walked some of that crap out of my lungs, I'd be better off for it. I stopped in the train shop on my way down Main Street, but the new Lionel cars weren't out yet, so I left and walked across the bridge. I was the only one at the office and it took an hour to sort through my mail from the last three or four days. My files were in shambles on my desk, so I started to stack those.

Mike Gmoser came in later that afternoon. We called Dan Fischer, who was cutting the grass, to join us. Since Dan was Catholic, and Mike used to be Catholic, I sent both of them down to St. Ann's Church and Sacred Heart Church to interview the priests. Unfortunately, they came back with the news that Father Baker at Sacred Heart didn't know Leonard Ruppert that well. In fact, he didn't know him at all, even though Leonard went to church every Sunday. And the priest at St. Ann's said he didn't know Charity

Ruppert. So we struck out on that. That would have been a beautiful plan, but we couldn't use it.

I worked on my questions for Dr. Mechanick, another Ivy Leaguer the defense brought in to say Ruppert was a paranoid schizophrenic. That would give us three different diagnoses in this case by their doctors. Grinspoon said he was suffering paranoia. Sokolov said he was suffering a paranoid condition. And Mechanick thought he was a paranoid schizophrenic.

I couldn't deal with Mechanick in his own ballpark, so I had to come up with some tricky business again. The first thing I planned to ask was whether he recognized Grinspoon as an authority on mental illness. I was sure he'd say yes. There was another thing I planned to ask him about from a Grinspoon article. Grinspoon wrote that psychomotor tasks in schizophrenic patients are easily differentiated from other patients. In other words, schizophrenics are much slower. I was going to ask him about that.

Mechanick was the defense's authority on schizophrenia and had only written four articles since 1964. They were "The Community Psychiatric Hospital and its Therapeutic Significance," "Is Psychiatric Hospitalization Obsolete?," "New Concepts in University Community Mental Health Services," and "Non-Medical Drug Use Among Medical Students." The articles had nothing to do with mental illness. I planned to spar with him a little bit about that.

On the way home that night, I stopped at the pizza house and ordered a pizza. That was what my son John wanted and I did too. Then I walked the 15 minutes to my house and drove back to pick up the pizza. It was ready by then. Smart, huh?

Chapter 31

Join Holcomb
Monday, June 23, 1975

Everything was finally catching up with me. I worked till midnight last night and had never been so tired in all my life. I didn't know how long I could stand these hours. I snapped at Judy because the black suit she took to the cleaners had a broken hanger and the pants were all wrinkled, so I couldn't wear them. And she forgot to get gas for the blue station wagon. I called her later and apologized. I was nervous as hell and upset when I got to court. But by the time the bailiff banged the gavel on the desk, I was ready to go again.

When Dr. Mechanick took the stand, he testified that he interviewed Ruppert three times and never questioned the truthfulness of what he said. He said Ruppert shot his family reflexively. The only thinking and contemplation involved was, as the defendant put it, he couldn't stand the "moaning and groaning" from the victims and felt he should put them all out of their misery. The doctor said Ruppert did not know the difference between right and wrong and was unable to control his actions.

Judge Cramer asked him a bombshell of a question, which he surely did not field very well.

"Doctor, if all of these things occurred and if the defendant had no guns in his possession, what would he have done?" Cramer asked.

The doctor said he would not have done anything. I think they dropped a load in their drawers on that one on the other side of the courtroom. It seemed to me, as it would to any rational person, that if he flew into a psychotic rage, especially in the kitchen, he would have grabbed a knife or a frying pan or a coffee cup or a chair leg or just anything. Another thing Mechanick said was that motor control was not affected, even though he diagnosed him as a paranoid schizophrenic.

The next defense witness was the highly credentialed Dr. Henry Bachrach. He said the defendant was paranoid schizophrenic, just as his boss, Dr. Mechanick said. Bachrach was the associate director of the outpatient service at the University of Pennsylvania. I asked who the director was, and he said it was Dr. Mechanick. So Dr. Mechanick was his boss, in other words. The boss, Mechanick, testified he was making $100 an hour, or $800 a day. Bachrach, on the other hand, was making $65 an hour. In Bachrach's case, he said the counsel for the defendant was paying the bill, so the arrangement differed. His total bill, he said, would be about $2,000.

Bachrach said Ruppert's IQ was in the top 20 percent of the population. I had a little bit of fun with him, because I couldn't argue in his language. He told the court about these special tests he administered that showed Ruppert's thinking was permeated with violent thoughts. One of the questions was, "What would you do if you were in a crowded theater and fire broke out?" Ruppert answered he was uncertain, because if he yelled "Fire!" everyone would stampede and lots of them would probably get killed. I asked what an appropriate response would be. The doctor said notifying an usher would be more appropriate. I thought calling the fire department would be the appropriate response. Well, anyway, who knows?

The next defense witness was the dependable Don Stevens, a local psychiatrist who earned his medical degree from the University of Nuevo Leon in Mexico. He practiced medicine in about ten different states but was only licensed to practice in Ohio at the time. He testified he had been in business ventures with Holbrock, who also represented him on a couple run-ins with the medical board here. He was going to start a hypnosis clinic at one time, but the Medical Association put the quietus on that and Holbrock represented him on that. Stevens testified that the "incipient start" of

Ruppert's mental illness was in 1960, with the actual start in 1964. I'll be damned if he didn't make that diagnosis of an "extremely rare form of paranoia," just as the man from Harvard before him did.

In 1967, I had cross-examined Dr. Stevens on the stand in a different trial: the Roscoe Barnett case. Barnett was accused of killing his landlady and pleaded insanity. Stevens had testified in that case that, "There is no test known to psychiatry by which you can examine a person now, presently, and determine what that person's mental condition or state was at any given previous point in time."

At the end of my cross-examination of Stevens, I stood in front of the witness stand, slowly turned, and walked back across the courtroom to the prosecution table.

"Hand me the Roscoe Barnett transcript," I said to Fischer.

Fischer handed me a legal transcript with long brown covers on it, and I made a big production out of opening it up. I knew Dr. Stevens remembered examining Roscoe Barnett, and he probably thought I was reading the question to him from the Barnett transcript. In reality, I was reading from a little piece of paper stuck inside a random transcript. Barnett was found guilty of first-degree murder, but the jury recommended mercy and he was sent away for life. He never appealed, so there was no transcript in that case.

"Isn't it true," I asked, "that there is no test known to psychiatry which you can administer now which accurately can determine a man's mental state at any previous given point in time?"

Dr. Stevens thought for a minute and requested that I repeat the question. So I repeated it.

"Isn't it true that there is no test known to psychiatry which you can administer now which accurately can determine a man's mental state at any previous given point in time?" I asked.

"That's right," Dr. Stevens answered.

"OK," I said. "Thank you very much, doctor."

Next on the stand was Detective Line. He went to see Ruppert in 1965 about the obscene phone call he'd made to the librarian, but that was all the defense brought up in regard to the incident. On cross-examination, I asked the detective if he had made threats to inform the FBI about Ruppert's obscene call. Line laughed out loud.

"Why that's ridiculous," he said. "I wouldn't do anything like that."

"As a matter of fact," I said, "didn't Ruppert deny making the call?"

Line said that I was correct; Ruppert denied making the call.

"Didn't you tell him, in substance, if he did it, knock it off and don't do it anymore?" I asked.

Detective Line said that was exactly right.

That ended the proceedings for the day. Around five o'clock, Harry McDaniel, the deputy sheriff from the jail, called over and told us that Bressler had just come to the jail with a Dr. Roberts.

"Oh, damn," I thought. "That's the guy who was here in the competency hearing."

Mike called the Holiday Inn and found out the guy's name was Dr. Leigh Roberts. He was in private practice in Madison, Wisconsin, had all his training at the University of Wisconsin, and was a professor of psychiatry there. Mike called the DA's office of Dane County and talked to their chief trial counsel, Jerry Lynch, who said the prosecution uses Roberts often and characterized him as a real straight shooter.

I took Mike home, not for supper, but to wait while I changed clothes. He sat on the back porch and drank a cold beer while Andy, my 7-year-old, told him about how he dives off the 20-foot diving board. I thought that was really great, because I was afraid to go off the damn thing until I was in high school. My daughter, Mary Ann, told him how she dives backward off the low board. Then Jeffrey wanted to hit a few baseballs, so I threw him a few and he hit them. All this took just a brief amount of time, then we went to the Homestead for a bowl of bean soup, shredded beef sandwich, and a Pepsi. We gulped it down and went back to the office to get ready for the next day.

I wasn't really that scared at that point because I didn't think we'd been hurt too badly by the defense case. I was just too damn tired to do much more than talk strategy, how it was going, and where we were going next. I didn't get much work done to prepare for Dr. Roberts, due to my exhaustion. I was just going to wing it. Janet came in and typed up a bunch of subpoenas for the next two days, and then we went home.

Chapter 32

JOHN HOLCOMB
Tuesday, June 24, 1975

I woke up at six o'clock the next morning, got ready and drove to work. I momentarily fell asleep waiting for a traffic light downtown. I was ready to go again when I got to the office. I took a Valium and tried to relax for a little bit before it was time to go back to court.

It was going to be a short day. The court was going to adjourn at noon for a judicial conference in Cincinnati for the remainder of the week. When I got to court, I noticed the row of seats right behind our counsel table was absolutely empty, except for my secretary Fran. She had a big smile on her face as she sat there by herself, and that touched me. I really appreciated her loyalty. She had been kind of a regular at the trial, attending about half the time. Mary Sue Predit, another secretary who was off in the summer, also attended a couple of days. She was there Monday with her husband, Dave. That's how loyal those girls were. They hung right in there with me, and it made me feel better to see them there.

Dr. Glenn Weaver was the first witness of the day. He was the doctor who saw Ruppert between 1961 and 1964. Weaver testified that Ruppert suffered from "paranoid type disorder, paranoia," and had an IQ of 125. He went through the same general routine as the other psychiatrists. I set him up real nice. First, I had him concede that, back in the early '60s, he was treating Ruppert for neurosis of a masochistic character, which is a far cry from psychosis. Then I had him elaborately describe how difficult it is to diagnose a psychosis, what tests are involved, personal interviews and this and that. Then I whipped out the letter that he had written in 1961 to Dr. Rond in Columbus, referring Ruppert to him. He had outlined some of

Ruppert's problems in the letter. He also stated in the letter that Charity Ruppert was psychotic.

"You wrote this letter, you tell me how hard it is to diagnose psychoses, and here's a lady you've never seen before and you called her psychotic to another physician," I said.

"That's all," I added, and sat down.

Made a real big score.

Then the defense called Dr. Roberts and spent an hour and a half on his credentials. He graduated from the University of Illinois and taught psychiatry at the University of Wisconsin Medical School. He was on so many damn boards and committees and clinics, I didn't see how he had time to practice psychiatry. We started in on Dr. Roberts around eleven o'clock, and about ten minutes after twelve, Judge Cramer said we needed time to eat and declared a recess until one o'clock.

During recess, I approached Dr. Roberts in the hall and introduced myself.

"I just wanted to shake your hand and tell you I talked to Jerry Lynch up in Madison about you, and he said you're good friends and you're as straight as an arrow," I said to him. "I want you to know that you and I are going to bump heads in here, but I think a lot of you, as long as you are a buddy of Jerry Lynch's."

"Oh yes," he said, "I think very highly of Jerry. Where do you know him from?"

I said I met him at a district attorney's convention in Chicago last summer, and we had skipped the last day to go to the racetrack together.

He laughed and said that sounded like Jerry.

Now, I didn't know Jerry Lynch from the man in the moon, but my strategy was that Dr. Roberts might not go so damn wild in his testimony down here if he knew I could make a phone call to Lynch and maybe cut him out of a big bundle of work. I think it worked, too, because his testimony could have been a hell of a lot worse.

When we came back, Roberts went through Ruppert's entire life history until quarter till four. When the defense had him do this, I was positive Ruppert would not take the stand. In 1962, he left home. In 1963 he went back home for a weekend and saw his mom searching through his clothes and going through his billfold. In 1964, he was a failure in school, work, and in his social life. In 1965, a librarian told him he must sure have an exciting life if he was always in the library. It upset him so much he called her up and called her a fucking bitch. Then the police officer, Detective Line, went to see him and told him to knock it off.

In 1967, over in Indianapolis, Ruppert was a big stock market player. Somebody at the stock exchange told him, "Your stock sucks." Shortly after that year, he went to Florida and a fortuneteller told him that people were saying he was crazy behind his back. Then he got the idea: "Dimple in chin, devil within." His thinking gradually deteriorated to a belief that all his ideas started with the President of the United States. In 1970, he called a company in Cincinnati, and heard someone say in the background, "Oh, you're his brother." He got the idea that they had already been in touch with Leonard.

By 1973, there was a larger series of events. He was sure people in a restaurant were talking about him and were part of the conspiracy. His brother was sabotaging his car. Somebody pried open his strong box. His coworkers wanted him to commit suicide. The doctor took three hours to go through all this. He believed Ruppert was paranoid schizophrenic.

I got the doctor to admit that he was in Hamilton for $300 a day, which would make him a minimum fee of $1,800. It was only after I started bringing up the money that the witnesses started forgetting what the fees were. He said Ruppert was a "candid reporter," or absolutely truthful. During cross-examination, I asked him if Ruppert told him about waking up in bed with his mother in a compromising position. He said yes. I asked, "Did he tell you he was a homosexual?" He said Ruppert had described a homosexual incident to him. I asked if he confided that his brother fought all his battles for him. He answered no to that question.

Roberts also testified that the defendant came downstairs in a state of relative calm on the day of the murders. Then he had a conversation with his brother about the stock market. When Leonard asked about his Volkswagen, Ruppert flew into a "psychotic rage," as he called it.

"Doctor, what conversation did he have with his brother before he went up the stairs?" I asked.

At that point he became very general and evasive and said he really didn't know, but it was just general conversation. He said when he went into this psychotic rage, he became an even better shot than he ordinarily was. "Robotlike," to use his term. He testified on direct examination that he had inquired into the defendant's financial condition and found it to be a stable one for a number of years and that he had reasonable success in the stock market. I asked him if he categorized the "candid reporter's" financial situation as a stable one.

"Well, I'm not sure that I used that term," he said.

"Well, I think you did," I said.

"I'm not so sure I did," he said.

"Doctor, did the 'candid reporter' tell you that between January 1971 and January 1975, with Merrill, Lynch, Pierce, Fenner & Smith, he invested $28,000 and lost it all?" I asked.

He looked at me for a minute and answered, "No."

"Thank you very much, Doctor, and have a pleasant trip back to Wisconsin," I said.

I could hear the reporters buzzing in the jury box. I always liked that sound because I knew I'd scored with dynamite. That was how the day ended, and the defense indicated they were going to rest. They were not going to put Ruppert on the stand. Judge Cramer let them go over until tomorrow morning before they rested, so we would have our rebuttal witnesses there and ready to go first thing.

There was a message on my desk back at the office that Mrs. Skalkos called and said she did not want to be a witness. The message said she could not swear to the fact that the two Ruppert brothers were in her restaurant eating together. It was a blow to me, because I was going to have a mess with Mrs. Skalkos. I asked every psychiatrist what Ruppert did the Saturday before Easter. And they all said he went out drinking that night. Well, hell yes he did, but I wanted the judges to hear what he did in the daytime. He had an argument with his brother down in Skalkos's Restaurant. Incidentally, Dr. Roberts testified that Ruppert's last contact with his brother before Easter was in January, to negotiate a note.

I suspected what happened with Mrs. Skalkos had something to do with the fact that she was of Greek descent and had been in the restaurant business in town for many, many years. George Jonson, Hugh Holbrock's law partner, was also Greek, and his father had been in the restaurant business on High Street, just like Mrs. Skalkos. I wondered if George Jonson went down to see Mrs. Skalkos and put a little heat on her about testifying? After I had asked the psychiatrists that question, I knew damn well that Bressler or Holbrock went back to the jail and asked Ruppert what he did Saturday during the day. I was sure he told them about having breakfast with his brother and having an argument with him.

So that was what we needed to iron out.

It was an amazing thing that when I came in that morning, I was so damned tired I fell asleep at that traffic light down on the corner, getting ready to turn into the jail parking lot. Just for 30 seconds or so. But after I had some coffee, I was OK. After the day was over and we were able to turn it around—at least a little bit—I perked up. Mike was all worked up, and Jocko was all worked up, but we were ready to go until midnight, one, or two o'clock in the morning again. I would worry about getting my sleep after tomorrow. We needed to get this baby rolling and figure out where we were going.

I went home to change my clothes, and little Jeffrey wanted me to play ball with him. I let him hit a few out in the backyard. That kid was going to be a great ballplayer. I had the little guy throwing right and batting left. And he really had the talent for it. Little

Andy came running up and told me about how he was turning somersaults off the high dive, so I patted him on the back and told him I was afraid to go off the high dive until I was in high school. Little Mary Ann, my pretty little girl, told me she was able to dive and turn somersaults off the low diving board. Then John came up and wanted to know how the trial went. I told him as much as I figured he could understand. Then he showed me two targets with some pretty good shot patterns in them. He was going out to the farm with Uncle Tom every day, and he took his rifle out with him.

The kid was going to grow up to be a hunter, no question about that. When John was only 3 years old, my dad bought him a .22 rifle, a little carbine rifle. I thought it was because he wanted to make sure he bought one of his grandsons a gun before he passed away. My Dad was a great hunter, too. That was something our family always did together. I did it with my boys, too. I was breaking them in. When John was 7, Uncle Tom gave him a .410 shotgun and I'll be damned if we weren't rabbit hunting out on the farm on Thanksgiving Day, which we always did for the past 30 years. We were walking through the fields and all of a sudden Dad spied a rabbit and told us to stop. The rabbit was sitting up in a clump of grass, and Dad motioned for John to walk up closer to it. John lined that .410 up on him and he had trouble steadying the gun; the end of the barrel was wavering. Dad said you better hurry up and shoot it, I can't take much more of this. John pulled the trigger. His first shot with the .410, and he got himself a rabbit at 7 years old.

Later, Mike, Glenn and I had supper at the One High Club, because we felt so good about the day's events. For the three of us, the bill came to $31, and I made up my mind I was going to pay for all my meals at night, since I was working ungodly hours, out of the Furtherance of Justice Fund. I supposed the state auditors would bitch about it, but if they did, I'd tell them to kiss my big you-know-what.

Chapter 33

JOHN HOLCOMB
Wednesday, June 25, 1975

My young neighbor Amy Smith, the daughter of lawyer Neil Smith, and her friend Betsy Davidson, the daughter of my dear friend Elmer Davidson, a lawyer who passed away, came to watch the trial today. The two middle-school girls were going to bring my son John with them, but he decided to go swimming instead. I took Betsy in to see Judge Cramer and introduced her as Elmer Davidson's daughter. I was overwhelmed to be holding this girl's hand, and I got tears in my eyes just thinking this was my late friend's daughter. I wished Elmer could have been there to see it. I knew he was at that bar association up in the sky with a good cold Hudepohl in his hand, looking down on us and having a real big laugh.

The day started with the defense resting. We offered the Grinspoon article and Dr. Weaver's letter to Rond into evidence. Then we offered the sunset and weather reports from the day of the murders. The defense jumped straight up and down on that, but Judges Cramer and Marrs conferred, and Fiehrer agreed, to admit them. We put on employees from Hayden-Stone to testify that Ruppert came to their office often and seemed to be of sound mental health. We put on Joan Fatika, the librarian who testified she had known Ruppert for 10 years from his regular visits to the library. In fact, Ruppert was there on Good Friday. We put on Dean Cavett, of the coin and gun shop, and he testified Ruppert seemed completely sane.

We put on Detective Paul Line, and he testified he knew Ruppert when they were boys. Growing up, Line said, Leonard Ruppert always fought his brother's battles for him. And even though they lived in the front part of a barn, it was fixed up with linoleum on the floor and kept nice and neat. Line said the Ruppert boys did not have the best clothes, but they were always clean. I tried to put Ebbing on the stand to testify as to their conversation after Ruppert invoked his right to remain silent, but the court did not permit that. I also tried to put on Terry Malone, the vice principal of Badin High School and Ruppert's old locker-mate, to offer Ruppert's high school records, but the court did not permit that, either. I interpreted that as a good sign, signifying the court was in our corner and did not want error in the record that would require reversal of the case by the Court of Appeals.

We called Bea Carr, who gave me a long statement, all of her own volition, back in April. She had walked in the office and told us what a good friend of the family she was. She was "backing water" terribly. She told me on the phone that everything in her statement was true, how terrible the Rupperts were and that kind of business. Charity Ruppert used to prance around the house naked and say the body was nothing to be ashamed of, Bea told us. I was scared to death of what she might say. I put her on the stand to testify that Ruppert sent her three letters from the jail and that they showed normal and sane thought processes, unlike the zombie he appeared to be in the courtroom.

Mike and I debated whether or not to put on Edna Skalkos. He was convinced we should do it, so we sent Detective LoBuono down to serve her to come to court forthwith. She refused to go, saying her attorney advised her she did not have to testify. I advised the court of this, and the court sent Detective LoBuono back to pick her up and bring her to court. We put her on the witness stand and she testified that she thought she saw James and Leonard Ruppert come into Skalkos Restaurant the Saturday before Easter. The smaller one (James) ordered donuts and coffee, and the taller one (Leonard) walked up to the counter and told her to cancel the donuts and make it two large orders of sausage and eggs instead. She also testified that the larger Ruppert (Leonard) was gesturing with his hands in a "So

What?" or "I don't have any more money" attitude. The smaller one (James) was just sitting there staring at the table, she said.

On cross-examination, Holbrock jumped up and asked her if the prosecutor came down to her restaurant and harassed her, tried to tell her what to say, and put words in her mouth. She said no, he didn't. That was the end of that. All in all, I thought she was a most effective witness, because it was perfectly obvious to the judges that Ruppert did, in fact, go to Skalkos Restaurant with his brother the day before the murders.

Court adjourned at 11 a.m. I gave Mike complete charge of going through the financial records and presenting that part of the case. Our records from Merrill, Lynch, Fenner & Smith showed that Ruppert lost $28,000 between January 1971 and January 1975. If we didn't prove that after the big deal I made, we would fall flat on our faces.

We called for Sgt. Dick Carpenter, who conducted the search of the house, to come talk to us. He advised us there were still some books and papers in the house. So I sent Glenn, Mike and Carpenter to go through the house again. They came back with a big paper sack full of stuff. They found a book, *Games People Play*, by Eric Berne MD, which had transactional analysis and psychiatric terms in it. They found a piece of paper in Charity's handwriting that read: "Marty Shepard, 9:45 p.m.—Tear up that traffic ticket. He has fixed it. He just saved you $17. I thanked him. Wednesday, p.m., May 27."

I found that fascinating and intriguing. Dick Carpenter was going to check out all the traffic tickets issued on May 27 for the past several years. Wouldn't it be something if it turned out that James Ruppert went to the conspirators—the police—to have a traffic ticket fixed? I had faint hopes for it.

We also found an identification card for Detective Don Noes (who was stationed in the house the night of the murders and drew the diagram of the bodies). On the back, in Charity's handwriting, it said "June 25, 1974, about 2:45 p.m." When we saw that, we could not figure out why Noes would have occasion to be at Ruppert's house last June, a year before the murders. We called Noes, and he said he didn't even remember being there, but he would review his daily records. His records showed he went to 635 Minor Avenue to investigate a vandalism complaint filed by James Ruppert. I could have died when he told me that. Noes looked up the report and called back half an hour later. He located a complaint filed by James Ruppert, 635 Minor Ave., at 11:30 p.m. on June 22, 1974. The officer who received the complaint was Patrolman S. Collins.

"Mr. Ruppert reports that sometime between 4:30 p.m. and 9:30 p.m., 6/22/74, someone used an unknown object to dent in the passenger side hood of his blue '68 VW sedan, Ohio license 1685 MA, while it was parked in front of The 19th Hole, Hamilton Plaza," according to the report.

The report continued: "Mickey Cornett is the barmaid at The 19th Hole—Ed Carlson is her boyfriend. Mr. Ruppert believes that Mickey put her boyfriend up to damaging Mr. Ruppert's car. Two days ago, Mr. Ruppert took sides in an argument between Mickey and another patron at The 19th Hole."

Now that had dynamite in it. Mickey Cornett was going to be one of our best witnesses as to Ruppert's sanity and how well she knew him. We had an ethical obligation to make the other side aware of this complaint instead of just saying, "Look what we've found." I was just going to offer the damn thing into evidence because it was a two-edged sword. The side that hurt us was that it showed Ruppert was, arguably, paranoid. He thought somebody was trying to damage his car and thought this Mickey Cornett put her boyfriend up to it. The part that helped us was, first, there was definite damage to his car. Second, he didn't think Leonard was responsible. Third, he called the police. Fourth, he didn't tell his damn psychiatrist about it. So, I thought, all in all, it was going to operate much more in our favor than against us. We were obligated to offer it into evidence, even if we lost the whole damn case over it.

I put Glenn Ebbing on this Mickey Cornett business. Glenn called and made arrangements to meet Mickey at a bar called

Maham's, which was in nearby Millville, to see if she knew anything about the incident involving Ruppert's car. He was going to ask her if she had an argument with a patron, and if Ruppert sided with the patron, two days before the vandalism. He also planned to ask if Mickey got mad at Ruppert and told her boyfriend, Ed Carlson, to kick in his car. Ebbing was working on that angle, while Mike worked the financial angle.

I had appointments with Dr. Thomas in Dayton and Dr. Fuess in Cincinnati. I needed to get the two doctors lined up in terms of their testimony. If we could come through halfway decently with our psychiatrists and the latest development didn't scorch us too badly, we would be in a much better position to know where we stood.

That was when a bombshell dropped. Dynamite.

Glenn came back from talking to Mickey Cornett at about 12:30 Wednesday night/Thursday morning. He had talked to her and drank a little beer with her. He brought a six-pack of Hudepohl back to the office for us to share. Mickey denied the incident that Ruppert related in his statement. I feared that would go against us by showing he really was paranoid. Mickey said she never had an argument with any patron in front of Ruppert, and as far as she knew, Ruppert never sided with anybody in anything.

Mickey related a story about a patron who drew a gun on another patron in the bar, and everybody hit the deck real quick—except Ruppert. He just sat there. After the trouble subsided, she said, everybody asked Ruppert why he didn't duck or run. He said he figured if his time was up, his time was up, and there wasn't anything he could do about it. Incidentally, his psychiatrist related that same incident in court. All this could damage our case.

Mickey told Ebbing the girl we really wanted to talk to was Wanda, because Wanda was "going" with Ruppert at the time. That was the first we'd ever heard of this. I went back through the witness statements to Don Noes about the VW vandalism incident. Mickey Cornett's April 2 statement said, "I know of no real close friends that he had, but on two or three occasions, which would be a while back, a woman would call him at the bar, and he would talk to her and I think her name was Wanda, but I don't know the last name and I don't know what their conversation was."

We needed this Wanda, and we needed to find her damn quick. At that point, we didn't even know her last name. She was the girl supposedly going out with the guy who hated women. Mickey said this Wanda worked at The 19th Hole for three or four days, and that was how she met Ruppert. She got fired, and Ruppert got upset about that, Mickey said.

Ebbing called Tom Farrell, the owner of The 19th Hole, and told him he needed some information on a former employee named Wanda who worked there for three days. Tom told him there wasn't any Wanda who worked there for three days.

"I don't care about the three days, pal, but I need Wanda bad," Ebbing told him.

What he meant was he didn't care about Farrell not keeping the tax records for his short-term employees. Farrell softened and said he was sure he wouldn't know where she lived.

"Pal, I want you to understand it good," Ebbing said. "I need her *bad*. You call me in five minutes and tell me where I can find her."

Then he hung up the phone.

By God, five minutes later the phone rang. Tom Farrell said all he knew was that Wanda lived at the Ada Lee Trailer Court. So we called the Ada Lee Trailer Court. By this time it was 1 or 1:30 a.m., and nobody answered. Then we called the sheriff's department and the sheriff said the manager of the trailer park was Gene Couch, and he gave us a phone number. So Glenn called the number and a woman answered and said nobody named Couch lived there. So I looked in the phone book under Gene Couch, and that was the same number Glenn dialed. I figured somebody was jacking us around. So I called the number, and a guy with a real Kentucky drawl answered.

"Is this Gene Couch?" I asked him.

"No," said the man with the drawl. "Who is this?"

I was mad, convinced the guy was lying.

"John Holcomb, Butler County Prosecutor," I said. "Who is this?"

"Bill Halcomb," he said.

"You got to be shitting me," I said.

"Who do you want?" he asked.

"I'm calling Gene Couch," I said.

I gave him the number I had for Gene Couch, and he confirmed that it was his number—not Gene Couch's. At that point, we looked in our respective phone books and discovered that the wrong number was printed in the phone book. The number listed for Gene Couch was really Bill Halcomb's phone number. I felt like a fool and apologized for being rude. He apologized in return and explained that he had been getting crank calls, which accounted for his suspicious demeanor. I asked him if he spelled his last name with an "A" or an "O," and he said it was spelled with an "A," a common Appalachian spelling of Holcomb (or Holcombe).

"After you get back across the Ohio River, I guess it's all the same, anyway," I told him.

He laughed and agreed. Then he asked what part of Kentucky my family came from. I told him Rockcastle County. He said he was from Livingston.

"Oh, God! That's where my grandfather's from!" I said.

So we talked a little bit and figured we probably were related in some way, even though we had never met.

So after that phone call, we went back to trying to locate Wanda. No luck. Ebbing poured me a Coke with a good stiff shot of Jack Daniels Green in it, making me more tired than ever.

"Don't worry," Ebbing assured me. "I'll come up with her in the morning."

And we all went home for the night. It was nearly three o'clock in the morning. I ate a ham sandwich and drank a glass of milk, leafed through a magazine on model railroads, and went up to bed. Young John was asleep in my bed again, and I was too tired to move him, so I climbed into his bed and slept there.

Chapter 34

JOHN HOLCOMB
Thursday, June 26 to Sunday, June 29, 1975

Judy woke me at nine thirty in the morning to tell me Glenn Ebbing was on the phone.

"Come to the office right away," Ebbing said. "I've found that girl."

I showered and shaved quickly and sped down to the office. There sat Ebbing, Sgt. Carpenter, and Mike—with Wanda Bishop. She had quite a story to tell.

Wanda said she fell in love with Ruppert after meeting him at The 19th Hole. They always met at the bar, although he did go to her trailer once. She knew damn well that he wasn't a homosexual, because all he wanted to do was run his hands all over her body and try to get her to go to a motel with him, she told us.

On the Saturday night before Easter, at about two-thirty in the morning, Ruppert told her he was going home to get a problem settled with his mother. She asked what the problem was. He said his mother told him if he had enough money to go out drinking in the bars all the time, he had enough money to be helping out with rent.

That was her dynamite story. If we put that out there into testimony, and if Wanda didn't get chopped up too much by the defense, we were going to win the case. Now Wanda was plain, poor, ill-spoken, and 28 years old. She had false teeth, shaved-off eyebrows, a rail-thin physique and no education. Instead of saying "fight," she said "fit." Instead of "quarrel," she said "fuss."

We decided we would hide her out, because she might go back to The 19th Hole and let the cat out of the bag. Ebbing had been checking the records at Hamilton Municipal Court, and we feared some of those employees might let Holbrock know about her. We also feared some of Wanda's neighbors at the trailer park might tell her not to get involved in the matter, and just go back to Kentucky until the whole thing blew over.

We arranged to get a cabin at Hueston Woods State Park through Officer Broderick, who was one of the rangers. Broderick was the guy who came to report to my investigator, Cliff Hyde, on a weekly basis. The report wasn't for law-enforcement purposes, but to tell him where the bass were biting in Acton Lake up at Hueston Woods. We also lined up Nancy Martin, an Oxford Police dispatcher, to sit with Wanda day and night, right up until we put her on the witness stand Monday. We gave Nancy some money to fix Wanda up, buy her clothes and anything else she needed, and make sure she didn't get scared or wasn't bothered by anyone. This girl had no decent clothes, so Nancy bought her a pants suit at Grant's in Oxford. Nothing fancy, just something decent. Then they rented a TV to put in their cabin at Hueston Woods.

Some officers were going to buy groceries for the cabin, and they asked Wanda what kind of steak she liked. She said she'd never had steak in her life.

When the officers pulled up at the cabin in a detective car with their bags of groceries, there were a whole bunch of people in a cabin right across the way that recognized it as a police vehicle. The detectives thought it was funny as hell that these people across the way thought a bunch of policemen were shacking up with two women for the weekend. But they got Wanda all settled into that cabin in the middle of Hueston Woods. What we planned to do was march her right into that courtroom at nine o'clock Monday morning and hit them right between the eyes with her.

Jim Farquis stopped by the office around seven o'clock and we had dinner at Johnny Dallis's. Chicken and dumplings. We talked about the old days, old girlfriends and old fights. I ran into the coroner, Dr. Boone, on my way back to the office. He saw me coming down the street and pulled his car over. He said he was subpoenaed to go to a deposition in Kentucky and wanted to know if he had to attend. I told him not unless the subpoena came from the governor and the check for his expenses was enclosed with it. He said in that case he would skip it. That put me back at the office around eight thirty, and Dick Carpenter called in to say Wanda was all situated at the cabin and they were going to stop for a steak at the Rainbow Dinner House in Millville.

Later that night, my son John called me and asked if visitors were allowed at my office. He said they had just watched a movie at the Court Theatre down the street. I watched them leave the theater from my window. John, my son Andy, my daughter, Mary Ann, and our neighbor Amy Smith walked in around nine o'clock. They were looking through the suite of offices, and Andy climbed up in my desk chair, leaned back, put his feet up and said, "Now I'm a big shot." They stayed for about an hour.

After the kids left, we continued talking about the possibilities of how to use Wanda. Dan brought a 12-pack of beer with him, so we drank as we strategized. It was ten minutes till two when we walked out of the office with our plan.

On Friday, Dan and I went down to see our psychiatrist Dr. Feuss in Cincinnati. Dr. Feuss said he agreed with Grinspoon's articles that psychiatrists often disagree on diagnoses. He said the reason is because psychiatry is an art which attempts to use scientific methods. I asked him about the dream Ruppert had 15 years ago that he was going to be executed. Feuss said dreams mean absolutely nothing, unless they recur over a long period of time. He said he just went to see a movie called *Jaws*, and that night he dreamed that sharks were biting him in the ass.

We got Feuss all squared away. He believed Ruppert was paranoid state, and borderline psychotic, if you wanted to classify him as psychotic. Feuss said Ruppert knew what he was doing and knew the difference between right and wrong. As we were finishing up, I asked Dr. Feuss how much he was charging me. We had never discussed his fee.

"I'm charging you exactly the same amount of money the judges in your county pay court-appointed psychiatrists," he told me. (Court-appointed psychiatrists were paid far less than those retained by counsel.)

"You've got to be kidding me," I said.

"No," he answered. "That's the way I am."

He really was a magnificent man. Dan thought he was the most impressive doctor he had ever seen. I thought he was going to make all the Ivy League big wigs look like hell.

When Mike came back from going over the figures at Merrill-Lynch, he said we would have to revise them downward. That was what I was afraid of. Mike's computations showed that Ruppert lost $28,000 in four years, and Merill-Lynch's accountants figures showed he lost something like $22,800. Still a devastating blow to Ruppert.

One thing they discovered when they went through the house was an application for food stamps. That was going to lend a lot more weight to my argument. Here was an elderly woman, with a limited income and about to go on food stamps, who told her son if he had enough money to go out drinking in bars every night, he had enough money to help her pay the mortgage. It was the most logical thing in the world. I thought it would make a devastating argument.

We checked on Wanda at Hueston Woods, and she was still getting along OK. I just hoped we could keep the news under wraps. I stopped over at the jail on the way back from Cincinnati and asked to see the visitor list for Ruppert. Hoot Gibson, a deputy sheriff (I guess everybody named Gibson is called Hoot), said something that made me wonder.

"You guys made a little discovery, didn't you?" Hoot asked.

"Huh?" I asked.

He repeated his question. I played dumb.

"You've got the wrong dope on something," I said. "I don't know what you're talking about."

He just gave me a big wink, and then we went on with our business.

I thought I knew what happened. Nancy Martin was married to a deputy sheriff, and he probably went back to the sheriff's office and told his buddies his wife was babysitting a surprise prosecution witness in the Ruppert case. So that was probably where we stood.

I went back to the office and started writing questions for Dr. Feuss after Janet left at 5:30. Around 6:30 or 7, I felt somebody shaking me awake. It was Fran. She wasn't working over the summer, of course, but she still had keys to the office and stopped in to pick up her paycheck.

"You were sound asleep in that chair," she said.

I guess I'd been that way for an hour or more.

A little while later, the phone rang. It was Janet.

"Are you OK?" Janet asked. "You just didn't look good when I left, and I was worrying about you."

I told her I was OK, thanked her, and said I appreciated her concern. That was really touching and gratifying to me. I left the office after midnight, picked up a pizza on my way home and killed that while I watched some foolish show on TV. Then I went upstairs to bed. I hadn't weighed myself in a while, but I thought I'd lost 10 to 15 pounds in the last week or two. I hadn't been eating, hadn't been sleeping, and my pants (which were tight before) were so loose they fell to the floor when I unfastened my belt.

I woke up early out of habit and went back to sleep for a few more hours on Saturday morning. There didn't appear to be any breakfast again, and I didn't have time to wait. Little Jeff was all excited because Judy sent away to Shillito's department store to get him Pete Rose and Joe Morgan T-shirts. His favorite Reds players were Pete Rose, Joe Morgan (he called him Joe "Organ"), Johnny Bench, and Tony "Comprez" (his name for Tony Perez). I knew he was going to be watching the mail for the next couple days for those.

After I showered and shaved, I walked up to Ron's Barbershop on Eaton Avenue. Ronnie Crysel, the owner, was a friend of Fran and her husband. They were in a nice little group, so I always went to him to get my haircut. But his shop was filled up with customers, so I told him I'd catch him later.

I decided to walk to work. I walked down Eaton Avenue to Main Street and passed by Ray and Ernie's Barbershop. I had known those two fellows for a long time—ever since I was working as a mailman to pay for law school. I remembered carrying their mail way back in 1956. I used to go to Ray and Ernie when I was a kid. My time was too important to sit in a barbershop and wait for four or five guys ahead of me to get their haircut, so I ducked into Ray and Ernie's. I hoped Ron didn't get mad at me. It was the first time in 12 or 13 years I hadn't gone to him. He probably wouldn't know the difference, because I'm so "balding," to use a reporter's word. So I stopped in Ray and Ernie's place on Main Street, and Ernie cut my hair. Doggone if he didn't want to talk about 20 years ago when I played basketball on the state championship team. That made me feel like a million bucks. He asked me if I ever got a chance to play basketball anymore.

"Gosh, no," I replied. "I'm fifty pounds over my playing weight. If I ran out of this chair to the doorway, I'd die of a heart attack."

It made for a pleasant haircut. At least there are a few people who remembered I wasn't always a balding and chubby slob.

I continued on my way to work and saw my dad walking down the street just as I got to the Rentschler Building. I collared him and we went over to eat at Kosta's Restaurant and got some coffee to go. We sat in my office and visited for a while. Mike called to say he checked in with Wanda Bishop last night and she was happy as a bug in a rug out there at the cabin. The only thing she wanted was a fan to keep it cool, so we bought one for the cabin. Dr. Thomas—Dr. Dynamite Dan Thomas—came to my office around three thirty with an associate and stayed for three hours. Ebbing brought Mickey Cornett in at seven o'clock, and I talked to her for about three hours, trying to get the feel of the general atmosphere of The 19th Hole and verify what Wanda had told me. Another long day.

I left the office around eleven o'clock and started walking home. Detectives Noes and Philpot were driving by in their cruiser, but they were going in the opposite direction, so I just waved to them. Another block down, John Bohlen honked his horn at me. He was driving in the opposite direction, too, so I just waved. I walked across the bridge and saw Jim Craven, a patrolman, near the West Side Federal. He honked his horn at me and motioned. I ran across the street and jumped in his cruiser, and he gave me a ride home. Inside at home, I undressed and sat in my big red chair in my underwear and watched the late show on television for the first time in a long time. Then I fell asleep right there.

I woke up at 7 or 8 a.m., Sunday, and John came in to remind me that his tenth birthday was July 2. That was in three days. He said he wanted a telescope, which was really nice, except for the fact that it cost $200 plus. I knew the kids would just tear it up, so I talked him into getting a Schwinn 26-inch bicycle. He could wait until Christmas for the telescope.

I went to the office. Dan Fischer stopped in to say he was driving down to Lexington to talk to a lady about an estate I'd given him to handle. I told him as long as it didn't interfere with the murder case, it was all right with me. The estate was something we were handling together, and there was a nice fat fee in it for both of us. I wished him good luck. Then Mike and I drove to Hueston Woods to check on Nancy and Wanda. We went over her testimony. Wanda was going to be the first one on the stand Monday. That scared the hell out of me. Not that she wasn't honest. She was honest, but she was illiterate and her vocabulary was limited. She didn't know what "conversation" meant, but she knew what "talk" was. I was going to have to handle her with kid gloves. She called Ruppert "Rufford." I kept correcting her, but she kept saying "Rufford."

"That's how I knowed him," she said.

I asked her what she'd say when she went into The 19th Hole.

"Why, I said, 'Hi, thar, Little Jim,'" Wanda said.

If she came across like that in court, she was liable to kill us. I was just trying to get her to remember the magic sentence: his mother said if he had enough money to go out and drink seven days a week, he had enough money to help pay the rent, or else he could get out. So I kept drumming that into her head for about two hours. When Mike and I left, we were both still scared to death. We got a couple of bowls of chili and sandwiches from Frisch's and took the food back to the office.

I called Dr. Robert J. McDevitt. In his report, Dr. McDevitt said Ruppert knew the difference between right and wrong, but had an irresistible impulse. If he knew about Wanda Bishop and the rent problem with Ruppert's mother, would his opinion be different? He said absolutely yes. So the whole thing was going to turn on Wanda Bishop.

When I got home it was almost midnight. When I got into bed, Judy asked what I was going to do when the trial was over. I told her I'd like to take a few days off and go to a racetrack somewhere.

"What about us?" she asked.

"Well, I'll take you on a family vacation later in the summer," I said.

"I know you'll get busy and say you don't have time to go," she said.

"I'll take you anyplace you want to go," I told her. "Let's go to North Carolina and see my sister Mary Sue and her family."

Mary Sue's husband was a doctor down in North Carolina. Judy said she would settle for that.

"Just so I can tell the neighbors that we went somewhere," she said.

I told her that was what we'd do—not that I gave a good goddamn what the neighbors thought. So I guess she was going to let me take a few days off to go to a racetrack someplace, and then we'd take a week in August to take the family to North Carolina. God knows I could use a vacation. When I was young, I was too poor. Now, I was too busy. But I was determined to take one this year, no matter what.

Chapter 35

JOHN HOLCOMB
Monday, June 30, 1975

I got up at five o'clock and looked out the window. It was going to be a beautiful day. A beautiful, beautiful day. I got down to work about six, after I stopped over at Kosta's Restaurant and said good morning to Maud Fluckiger. She came from Rockcastle County, Kentucky, too. Her son, Simon, was a Hamilton Police officer. I frequently ate breakfast at Kostas, or sent the girls over for sandwiches. I got two large coffees with cream and sugar to go. I was still scared to death about Wanda Bishop. God, how she scared me. I could not imagine how the defense overlooked her. It was like it was too good to be true. She kept me on pins and needles. It was like handling a stick of dynamite that could blow somebody else up, but if you weren't careful, it could blow you up, too. I was so afraid of what she might or might not say, I was actually trembling and shaking. I said a silent prayer as I left for the courthouse.

When court started, the three judges entered and sat down at the bench. I walked to the doorway and gave Dick Carpenter a signal. He called on his radio for Glenn and Wanda, who were in a police car parked across the street at the county jail. We had to wait three or four minutes, and a great hush of anticipation filled the courtroom. She came marching through the door in the brand-new pantsuit we bought for her. Nancy Martin had given her a brand-new hairdo, too, so she looked better. In fact, she didn't even look like the same person. She marched right up and sat on that witness stand and told her story. She went over like a million dollars.

Wanda Mae Bishop testified she was in love with Ruppert and was with him the night before the murders. The mother of five said

138

she was separated from her husband and had been meeting Ruppert at The 19th Hole Cocktail Lounge every weekend and three nights a week for about eight months. She called him there quite a bit, too. Wanda said they'd never been intimate, but had engaged in necking, kissing and petting. He'd been to her trailer.

The Saturday night before Easter, they necked and kissed in the bar and the parking lot. He told her he had a problem that he had to settle right then with his mother. The problem, Wanda explained, was that his mother told him if he had enough money to blow in bars seven nights a week, he had enough money to help pay the rent—or he could get out. Ruppert had talked to her about his financial problems, his brother and his mother, she said.

Wanda testified that Ruppert left the bar around 11 p.m. and returned about half an hour later.

"I asked him if he took care of his problem, and he said, 'No, not yet,'" she told the court.

The defense was so shaken, they didn't know what to do. They were taken completely by surprise. They had a little index card system they used for background and witnesses. Her name wasn't even in the card index. Bressler asked her if she'd made a statement to the police or prosecutor. She said yes.

All the counsel went into Judge Cramer's office, and we played her tape-recorded statement. The tape wasn't even as good as her testimony, but there were no inconsistencies. Holbrock started raising hell with Mike Gmoser, because several times the tape clicked off and on, and Mike made a professional statement that he didn't add or delete anything from the tape. Holbrook lit into him and said he didn't think that was good practice, that we should have followed his practice of just letting the tape run regardless of what was happening. I'd heard enough of it.

"Hugh, I don't give a good goddamn what you think," I said. "I could care less."

Then we walked out of Cramer's office, and I heard Judge Marrs go, "Hmmmm," clearing his throat.

The defense cross-examined Wanda for about three minutes. Then she got down and marched right out of the courtroom. Our other witnesses were Lt. Ferdelman, keeper of the records at the Hamilton Police Department, and Officer Steve Collins, who took Ruppert's vandalism complaint on June 22, 1974. We were able to get into evidence that Ruppert's Volkswagen was damaged—not by his brother—but allegedly by Mickey Cornett and her boyfriend.

Mickey Cornett—Mary Ellen Cornett, the barmaid at The 19th Hole—took the stand next. She testified that Ruppert had been going to the bar about every day for the past six or eight months. She said he was friendly with people at the bar. He would buy them drinks, and they'd buy him drinks. She had seen him with Wanda and heard Wanda telephone the bar for him. Ruppert, she said, seemed sane, in her opinion.

Dick Carpenter testified next that he searched the defendant's car on April 1 and took stock market papers and books (including *The Games People Play*.) He also said he took a food stamp application filled out by Charity Ruppert. Those were accepted into evidence.

When I went back to the office at noon, I felt so good I couldn't believe it. Everything went off without a hitch. It must've been that silent prayer. I sat down in my chair and jumped right back up and started dancing on my toes. I wrenched the hell out of my back, pulled a muscle. Janet came running in. She got me halfway straightened out by the time we were due back in court.

Mike had a little bit of road trouble when he put on his financial experts from Merrill-Lynch. He hadn't gotten the stock records properly verified. Even though we got them into evidence, we had to proffer the amount of Ruppert's net loss in the last four years as $22,000. That was close enough, so we didn't have any problems with it.

Finally, I called Dr. McDevitt, the court-appointed psychiatrist. He testified that Ruppert had paranoid psychosis, knew right from wrong the night of the shootings, but could not resist the impulse to kill. I asked him the hypothetical question about his mother's ultimatum, and he said that would change his opinion.

We went back to the office and hashed it all over until about six o'clock. Judy and all the kids were just coming back from the swimming pool when I got home. She was getting ready to fix some spaghetti, but I didn't have time to stick around. I changed my clothes and told everybody so long. I got a bowl of chili, a mettwurst and a Pepsi at the Homestead, then stopped at the train shop and looked at a new Alaskan boxcar and a New York Central Pacemaker boxcar that had just come out. Then I went back to the office to get ready for the rest of the doctors' testimony.

JOHN HOLCOMB
Tuesday, July 1, 1975

I called Dr. Victor A. Thaler to the witness stand. The Dayton clinical psychologist had a bachelor's degree from City College of New York and a master's degree and PhD from Columbia University. He testified that after extensive testing, he diagnosed Ruppert as a "paranoid personality," which is not a psychotic condition. He felt Ruppert was mentally ill, but that the defendant did indeed know the difference between right and wrong and had the ability to refrain from shooting his family.

Next I called Dr. Dan Thomas, director of the Dartmouth Behavioral Sciences Center, in Dayton, and a graduate of the University of Parma, Italy, and the Marcy Institute in New York. He also had a fellowship to the prestigious Menninger Foundation at Topeka, Kansas. Thomas testified that he, too, thought Ruppert had a "paranoid personality" and was not psychotic. Ruppert "willingly" committed the crime, had the ability to refrain from doing so, and knew the difference between right and wrong, Thomas said. He also testified that there is no known test to determine a person's mental state at any time in the past.

Thomas said he thought Ruppert had convenient lapses of memory when it was in his own best interest. He also believed the repetitive firing and reloading of guns during the massacre showed the acts were willful, and not a reflex on Ruppert's part.

Dr. Thomas said never in his life had he seen a paranoid schizo-phrenic, or paranoiac, volunteer all the information that Ruppert did.

"A paranoid will never ask if you believe him," Thomas said. "He will actually become very distrustful. I thought it was unusual that he started relating about the conspiracy about an hour and a half after the interview started."

This was the subject of a lengthy cross-examination, but the defense did not shake him at all.

If Ruppert believed the conspiracy against him was widespread, he would not have continued to frequent places such as The 19th Hole, the library and Frisch's restaurant, Thomas said.

In the afternoon I called my big gun, Dr. Charles Feuss. He was from Beechwood, Kentucky, and graduated from Princeton University, got his medical degree at Vanderbilt and had taught psychiatry at Louisville, Marquette, the University of Cincinnati and Xavier University. He also was director of the Cincinnati Institute of Mental Health and chairman of the Cincinnati Medical Association's psychiatric committee for the past ten years.

The significance of Dr. Feuss was that he said a diagnosis of psychosis was not black and white; there is no fine line dividing psychosis and normalcy. He said there was a difference between being psychotic and being able to know the difference between right and wrong. He said Ruppert was psychotic, but in a gray area, and in good contact with reality. Ruppert knew the difference between right and wrong and had the ability to refrain from committing the act of murder, the doctor said. Feuss was dynamite. He also reiterated that he believed Ruppert's dream had no significance. Only dreams that recur for prolonged periods can be considered significant, he said.

On cross-examination, Bressler asked him if he had talked to him in the parking lot and told him this and that. Dr. Fuess asked if Bressler had tape recorded him, and he said yes. Feuss just started to shake and I thought he was going to have a heart attack.

"I feel this is very unethical," Feuss said. "I was talking to two ethical gentlemen, I thought."

At that point, I was convinced we had the case won, because there was a change in the atmosphere of the courtroom. I could see it in the judges. For the next hour, we called witness after witness who testified they knew Ruppert and considered him friendly, quiet, smart—and sane. Tommy Conese, who called himself "Papa Conese" and owned pizza parlors around town, said he'd known Ruppert 20 years. Laura Swisshelm testified that she saw Ruppert at a restaurant two days before the shooting, and he told her he'd met "a girl he could marry." Roy Tussey said Ruppert did everything in a very particular and painstaking way, including the way he spoke. He said one of Ruppert's hobbies was shooting, and described in detail how Ruppert had quick-draw target shooting down to a split second. I thought that was pretty devastating testimony.

After court, we went back to the office and strategized for Wednesday. We had about 15 witnesses left, but they would all give the same opinion that Ruppert was sane. We were at the high point in the trial, so I thought we should wrap it up real quick. We would end on a high note, I thought, even if it meant not calling 10 or 12 witnesses. Most importantly, we were going to force the defense to go ahead with its surrebuttal [response to opposing party] right away. The judges were tired of hearing this damn thing. They were not going to want to give the defense all day Wednesday and then have them start their surrebuttal on Thursday. I knew they'd be anxious to get this finished by the Fourth of July weekend. So we picked out our three or four best witnesses and planned to put them on first thing Wednesday.

JOHN HOLCOMB
Wednesday, July 2, 1975

Janet Feltner took the stand with two pictures of Ruppert taken at a party at The 19th Hole. In the background you could clearly see him necking with a woman at the bar. They had their arms around each other. That showed he wasn't the lonely little misfit sitting in the corner. He was right in there swinging with the rest of them, and he looked like he did pretty well for himself.

Our next witnesses, Kenneth Antal and Bill Ziegler, testified they knew Ruppert and considered him to be of sound mind. The last witness, Francis Pierson—one of the ideas I jotted down on a bar napkin while out drinking with Ebbing a week ago—testified Ruppert told him he did not believe in God. That shot holes in the defense argument that Ruppert didn't want to kill himself because he considered suicide a mortal sin. This was a guy who didn't believe in God in the first place.

Then we rested our case around nine thirty in the morning. Sure enough, the defense tried to get a continuance, but couldn't. That tickled us to death. We knew they had to try and destroy Wanda Bishop, and every hour was precious. They were going to run up and down the alleys and visit the joints to find people to discredit her.

They called several witnesses who testified Wanda had a reputation for being untruthful. Jane Halcomb, a barmaid at The 19th Hole, said she distinctly remembered Ruppert being at the bar the night before Easter, but said Wanda Bishop was not there. She had never seen Wanda Bishop, never knew a Wanda Bishop, and had never seen Ruppert with a girl. On cross-examination, I got her to admit she'd seen Ruppert dance with girls and she'd even danced with him herself. She even said he was a good dancer.

The defense brought on Elmer Bishop, Wanda's husband, who said he'd been served with divorce papers last Friday. He was 20 years old (eight years younger than Wanda) and was her fourth husband. Wanda, he said, had five children from previous marriages. He testified that Wanda was home every night from the middle of February to the middle of May and didn't leave their trailer. That included March 29, the night before Easter. I could not shake him on cross-examination. He stuck right to his story, even though we had other witnesses who had seen Wanda and Ruppert together. Bishop said he heard Wanda place a call to The 19th Hole after she'd heard about the murders, asking if Ruppert had been in the last few nights.

Elmer's mother, Eliza Bishop, also testified that Wanda was untruthful. Donna Gabbard, a barmaid at The 19th Hole, testified that Wanda had a reputation as an untruthful "trouble causer," and bar owner Tom Farrell said he'd only seen Wanda at the tavern once or twice since he fired her the previous year.

The defense wrapped it up with Shirley Klems, a good friend of Alma and Leonard Ruppert. She testified that Leonard Ruppert had a violent temper and had once thrown a spoon at her. On cross-examination, I asked her if Alma told her that Leonard was mad at his brother James. She said yes. I asked her if the reason he was mad was because James was 41 years old, not working, living off his poor mother (who was on a fixed income and preparing to go on food stamps), and he, James, was out carousing all the time. She said that was correct. That was the verification for Wanda Bishop right there.

The defense ended on that note. It was early afternoon, and I went back to my office to work on my final argument. I got a sandwich and a couple of Cokes, and I got everybody out of there. I wasn't taking any calls, but Janet said Judy called around noon. I asked if she was worried about the case. She said no; she wanted me to put $200 in her checking account because she just bought John a five-speed bike for his birthday today. So it was John's 10th birthday, and I couldn't even pick out his bike for him. I went home around suppertime, and they were getting ready to have a party for him. I didn't even have time to stick around, because I had to get back to work and finish my final argument. It made me feel terrible. But, thankfully, John didn't care. He got his new bike and didn't even miss me.

When I got back to the office, I told everybody to get the hell out and just leave me alone. I started working on my final argument at three o'clock in the afternoon, and I worked on it until three o'clock in the morning. I went over and over and over it. I could have argued all day if I put in everything that needed to be said. But the judges had set a two-hour limit. So after I was satisfied with my final argument, I went home and got three or four hours of sleep.

Chapter 36

As the trial neared its end, reporter Ken Bunting (who had previously described Holcomb as "chubby and balding") wrote about the lighter moments of the two-and-a-half-week proceedings. In the July 3, 1975, issue of *The Cincinnati Post,* Bunting characterized the Ruppert trial as "a courtroom spectacle" that at times "seemed as much like a Vaudeville act as a legal exercise."

The spectators who filled the courtroom's 56 wooden theater seats and lined its walls often burst into laughter at racy testimony or wry jokes from the lawyers and judges. For example, when defense witness and auto mechanic Elmer Bishop described first meeting his wife, Wanda Bishop, she couldn't afford her much-needed auto repairs. Mr. Bishop said he allowed her to "pay it off in trade." Holcomb asked him to elaborate, and Bishop explained the adult terms of their agreement, to the amusement of the gallery.

At other moments, "the often-rapid courtroom dialogue" ground to a halt more than once when court stenographer Margaret Spoerl stopped the action so she could capture every word in her notepad. Snickers could be heard whenever she did so. Spectators also chuckled when it appeared that Judge Cramer had dozed off in his chair. Cramer later admonished reporters for misrepresenting his state of consciousness. When he leaned back with closed eyes, he was simply "visualizing the evidence," he told them.

At another point, Judge Cramer's eyeglasses slid down his nose and landed on the floor. At the moment he disappeared to retrieve them, Judge Marrs leaned over to confer with Cramer, started to speak, and then looked quizzically at the empty chair. Again, the audience snickered.

Holbrook, always the showman, wore hand-tailored Western suits to court every day and referred to them as his "trial clothes." Some residents even saw the defense attorney driving Ruppert's infamous VW around town. In one exchange, Holbrook promised to jump out the courtroom window if he was in error as to a legal point. Holcomb walked over and raised the sash, explaining, "I wouldn't want you to damage county property."

Some testimony elicited uncomfortable silences and raised eyebrows among the spectators, especially when expert witnesses discussed Ruppert's "masturbation problem," impotence, and his one homosexual experience, according to the article. It was a typical small-town Midwestern response during the summer of 1975. The Vietnam War had come to its messy end, the blockbuster film *Jaws* was breaking cinematic records, and kidnapped heiress-turned-bank-robber Patty Hearst had made the FBI's Most Wanted list. In Hamilton, Ohio, however, the Ruppert trial consumed the imagination of its residents, who hungered for any details about the case, no matter how inconsequential.

Chapter 37

A total of 91 state and defense witnesses had testified, and more than 200 exhibits had been admitted into evidence. On Thursday, July 3, 1975, the time had come for closing arguments. Both sides spoke passionately, alluding to witness testimony, physical evidence and even Biblical passages.

Holcomb characterized the massacre as "murder for money," arguing that Ruppert planned and carried out the slayings to leave himself sole heir to the $300,000 family estate.

A motive "as ancient as the first reported murder case in the history of mankind —jealousy, envy, greed, and hatred"—drove Ruppert to kill his brother, mother, nieces and nephews, just as Cain slew Abel, the prosecutor said.

The details of the murders themselves showed premeditation and an acute awareness of reality on Ruppert's part, Holcomb argued. Ruppert had asked a friend about silencers. Ruppert had loaded his guns with hollow point "dum dum" bullets, which expand inside tissue to incapacitate and inflict maximum injury. Ruppert walked downstairs with every weapon he owned, fully loaded—including two tucked into his waistband—flouting the most basic gun-owner protocol.

"He knew he would have to run from room to room to accomplish his bloody task," Holcomb said.

The adults were all shot with "the powerhouse," the .357 Magnum revolver, while the children were shot with the less powerful .22 caliber gun, Holcomb said. And all but two of the victims had head wounds, in addition to their body wounds, which indicated Ruppert knew which people needed to be shot again. The rifle leaning against the refrigerator was a backup weapon in case someone tried to run from the house. In addition, the weather that day was freezing, with 20-mph wind gusts, low visibility and snow flurries.

"There was never any target shooting anticipated in this case," Holcomb said. "The only target shooting anticipated was on his family."

Ruppert wiped out 600 years of human life expectancy in a hail of well-placed bullets. "The question is, does the defendant pay, or does he *get* paid?" the prosecutor asked.

Bressler, on the other hand, argued that Ruppert was insane, acted in an uncontrollable "psychotic rage," and did not know the difference between right and wrong when he gunned down his family members. Expert witnesses—some of the nation's most eminent psychiatrists—corroborated this diagnosis.

"The delusion that Ruppert did this to inherit his brother's estate is only slightly less impressive a delusion as is Ruppert's delusion of a conspiracy," Bressler said, alluding to Dr. Grinspoon's testimony.

"The very act of killing eleven people is insane," he added, calling the slaughter "the greatest human tragedy that has ever occurred in these United States."

The attack was spurred instantaneously by Leonard's off-hand comment about the Volkswagen. "But for one remark made to an intensely sick man, we wouldn't be here today," Bressler said.

The defense characterized Wanda's testimony as perjury from a discredited source.

Holbrock followed with his summation, arguing that not "one scintilla" of evidence suggested Ruppert planned the murders for financial gain, or even knew how much his brother was worth.

"If those eleven people would arise from the dead and stand before you, they would say, one by one: 'Judges, acquit him.'" Holbrock said. "He is not guilty by reason of insanity, for he knew not what he did."

Dan Eichel, a prosecutor's office summer intern hired just three weeks before the trial began, sat behind the three prosecutors during the entire proceedings. The closing arguments, he said, remain his most vivid memory.

"I was a 23-year-old kid from a small Hanover Township farm, still baling hay on weekends with my dad in June 1975, fresh out of my second year of law school, into the office that was prosecuting this monumental case," Eichel recalled. "I had never seen *any* trial before, let alone the longest, the most significant trial of my career, let alone my lifetime."

Eichel spent the next 30 years prosecuting criminal cases and writing appeals, and not a single closing argument topped the one Holcomb gave that day, he said. Parts of it remained etched in his mind, such as the prosecutor waving the 11 police reports from the victims high above his head and throwing them "with a crash" into a strategically placed waste basket. He asked the judges if they would dare throw away 600 years of human existence without holding Ruppert accountable. He also remembered Holcomb borrowing Dox Quixote's words about the nature of madness: "When life itself seems lunatic, who knows where madness lies? Perhaps to be too practical is madness. To surrender dreams—this may be madness. Too much sanity may be madness—and maddest of all: to see life as it is, and not as it should be!"

Randy Rogers, who worked that summer as a law clerk and investigator for the defense team, echoed Eichel's sentiment, but added that the closing arguments "on both sides" were the finest he ever heard during his more than 40 years as an attorney and judge.

With closing arguments over, the crowd slowly drifted away, and the three-judge panel withdrew to deliberate the fate of James Urban Ruppert.

Chapter 38

The three judges deliberated for nearly four hours before announcing they had come to a decision. The principals were notified, and Ruppert was led across the street from the jail. A crowd of about 150 watched as deputies escorted the handcuffed prisoner back to the courthouse.

Ace Elliott, a reporter for the *Dayton Daily News*, heard a young woman wearing "a skimpy, short dress" yell, "Bring him out! We'll lynch him!"

Ruppert's Aunt Ruby Lee, who described herself as the defendant's only ally in the gallery, nervously waited inside the courthouse for her nephew to enter.

At 5:10 p.m., on July 3, 1975, with all the parties gathered, Ruppert looked up at the judges to hear their announcement. Judge Cramer read the verdict:

Guilty of all 11 counts of aggravated murder.

The defendant did not react but remained as stoic as he had throughout most of the testimony.

The judges voted 2-1 to convict as charged, with Cramer dissenting. Because the verdict was not unanimous, the death penalty seemed unlikely. Life in prison would be the probable sentence, but that would be decided after an investigation and a separate hearing, to be held within 30 days.

Holcomb expressed his satisfaction with the verdict, while the defense attorneys appeared dejected.

"I did my best," Bressler said. "That's all I could do."

Holbrock said they would likely appeal, the basis of which would be the lack of a unanimous verdict. That issue of a split verdict had not yet been resolved by the Ohio Supreme Court.

"The question will be squarely raised on whether or not a finding of this kind must be unanimous or not," Judge Cramer said.

Ruby Lee, when asked her reaction to the decision, could barely speak. She called the verdict unfair.

The crowd slowly dissipated after hearing the verdict. The marble floor outside the courtroom was littered with empty paper cups and candy wrappers, and stained with dried coffee and soda. At least for now, the show was over.

Chapter 39

John Holcomb
Thursday, July 3, 1975

Thank God for Judges Marrs and Fiehrer. That was the only thing I could say.

We got back to the office, sat around, drank a few beers and had a little celebration. Ebbing and Carpenter came over. Dan's brother Tom Fischer, Dan Connaughton (a former assistant prosecutor), Fran, Olga, Nancy and Janet were there. Ralph Bowman, president of the Fraternal Order of Police and the husband of my employee Sharon, called to congratulate me. Jim Farquis called from North Carolina to congratulate me, too. That got me thinking of our good friend Zeke Zimmerman, so I called him in Charlotte, and he said he'd already heard the verdict on the radio. My brother, Tom, showed up. Jim Irwin and his wife, Pat, came. Jim and Pat helped me a heck of a lot with the psychiatric part of the case. Pat was a psychiatric nurse.

I'd never been so tired in all my life. Just all worn out. I drank a few beers, but I certainly wasn't drunk or even close to it. Six or seven of us—including my law clerk Dan Eichel, Mike Gmoser, Dan Fischer and Glenn Ebbing—went down to the One High Club to get a late supper. The first thing I did was load up on a salad with some kind of rich, creamy dressing. Then I had the worst steak I'd ever had in my life. Then I started feeling kind of bad. I thought I'd feel better if I ordered dessert, so I topped all that off with a chocolate sundae.

Tom and Dan Fischer were singing Al Jolson songs at the bar when I walked out with Glenn and Dan Eichel and Mike. As soon as I got outside, I made a right-hand turn and walked back into the alley and puked my guts out. I wasn't drunk. I swear to God I wasn't drunk.

I was leaning against this brick wall back in the alley, vomiting, and I thought to myself how disgraceful it was to be doing this. I walked back out of the alley to my friends.

"Look, I'm so ashamed of myself," I said. "I apologize."

"What the hell, pal," Glenn said. "You're not drunk. It's not being drunk that caused that. I've seen you in a lot worse shape than that. That's all the tension and stuff coming out of you now. Come on. I know a good place we can go and keep on drinking."

"No," I told him. "I'm just so ashamed of myself. You guys go on. I'm going to go on home and go to bed."

It was eleven o'clock when I got home, and everybody was already in bed. I cleaned myself up, got under the covers, and went to sleep.

JOHN HOLCOMB
Friday, July 4, 1975

I woke up Friday morning and felt good. When I went downstairs I noticed a bottle of champagne and a note on the kitchen table.

"Congratulations, John," the note read. "You did a great job. Suzanne, Vicky, Dave, & Betsey Davidson."

It was from my buddy Elmer Davidson's widow and children. After reading that, it all came out. I sat there and cried like a baby for ten minutes. I felt a lot better after that, and I went upstairs and got myself cleaned up.

I told Judy I wanted to go to the racetrack, but she said she didn't want me to go. So I just decided to go back to the office and work all day on the Fourth of July. I stopped over at Mom and Dad's on the way and visited with them for a while. As I was leaving, I kissed them both.

"Thanks a lot, Mom," I said. "Thanks a lot, Dad."

That's all that was said. They knew what I was talking about and why I was thanking them. They sacrificed so much in their lives for me and my brothers and sisters. They didn't say any more, and neither did I. It was a real tender moment.

Back at the office, I started to clean up the Ruppert files and get my own personal files sorted out, so there would be some semblance of order in this place when Monday rolled around.

After I finished up, I went to New London Hills swim club for the first time. We had a family membership there for four years, but I'd never been. I watched my kids swim and saw Andy dive off the high dive. Mary Ann was a heck of a good swimmer; John was, too. John was afraid to go off the high dive but went off the low board. I stayed out there for about an hour and then I started to get nervous, so we left.

We stopped over at Glenn's, and he put some steaks on the grill. A few other couples joined us, and we all drank a couple of beers and ate a good meal. When Judy and I returned home, I decided I'd better go back into the office and do some work. But then I sat down in my red chair around eight o'clock and drifted off to sleep. When I woke up, it was after midnight. I just walked upstairs and got into bed.

JOHN HOLCOMB
Saturday, July 5, 1975

I decided to go the races. I got up at six-thirty, shaved, showered, and told Judy I was going to River Downs. She gave me the OK. I called Ebbing and Wayne Rose and told them I'd pick them up at noon. I ate breakfast at the Homestead, then went next door to Tom's Cigar Store and bought a Daily Racing Form. I was in my office by seven, and I sat and studied the entries for that day's races for five hours, almost as meticulously and painstakingly as I had assembled the case against Ruppert. Then I picked up Glenn and Wayne and went down to the racetrack. We were all in great spirits because of winning the trial. Out of ten races, I had absolutely no winners that day. So maybe, finally, everything was getting back to normal.

Chapter 40

Defense attorney Hugh Holbrock begged the court to spare Ruppert's life during the sentencing hearing on Monday, July 14, 1975.

"Gentlemen, death serves no purpose," Holbrock pleaded to the three-judge panel. "Only God can give a life. Let only Him take it. If he is spared his life, at least we will have remained a civilized nation, rather than returned to barbaric times."

"He has too much blood on his hands," said Holcomb, arguing for the death penalty.

Absent a death sentence, he asked that the judges make certain Ruppert would remain imprisoned for the rest of his natural life.

Also at the hearing was Don House, an Adult Parole Authority supervisor who interviewed Ruppert for a pre-sentencing report. House told the court that Ruppert initially appeared calm, intelligent and rational during their meeting. Later, he said, Ruppert began to sob and talked about the conspiracy against him.

Media and spectators eager to hear Ruppert's fate again filled the courtroom to capacity. Judge Cramer announced the court's finding at 11:25 a.m.

Ruppert was sentenced to 11 life terms, to be served consecutively, for the Easter Sunday murders of his widowed mother, brother, sister-in-law and eight nieces and nephews. Ruppert—wearing a short-sleeve shirt, tan slacks belted at his waist, a yellow tie and his trademark glasses—showed no emotion as his sentence was announced.

Cramer said the judges "feel we have ensured, insofar as the law now stands, (Ruppert's) remaining incarcerated for the rest of his natural life."

"If I decide to appeal, how long do I have?" Ruppert asked in a barely audible voice.

Cramer told him he had 30 days.

The imposition of a death sentence would have required unanimous agreement on the part of the judges. Instead, the judges found at least one "mitigating circumstance" that spared Ruppert's life. Under Ohio law, one such mitigating factor is psychosis or a mental deficiency deemed insufficient to establish an insanity defense.

The sentence made national news. *The New York Times* ran a story along with a photograph of Ruppert being led to the courthouse by a plaid-jacketed deputy. Ruppert's crime would remain the largest mass murder of the members of one family in American history until 1987. On December 22 of that year, Arkansas resident Ronald Gene Simmons wiped out 14 members of his immediate family and two former coworkers over a six-day period.

Ruppert was remanded to the Southern Ohio Correctional Facility in Lucasville. Although his first parole hearing was scheduled for 20 years down the road, Cramer predicted the mass murderer's release would be unlikely. He was right.

While Holbrock and Bressler appealed to a higher court, Ruppert was transferred to a prisoner processing facility in Chillicothe, Ohio— his first stop on the way to the penitentiary. On July 23, 1975, the mass murderer rode with Sheriff Carpenter, Detective Joseph LoBuono and reporter Dick Perry, who managed to wrangle permission to accompany the group as an observer. Perry—known for his mantra, "Never let the truth stand in the way of a good story," and his book, *Vas You Ever in Zinzinnati?*—wrote a story that appeared in *The Cincinnati Post* the next day.

On the ride to Chillicothe, Ruppert initially discussed teachers at Hamilton Catholic High School with LoBuono, his former classmate. Long periods of silence followed, punctuated by brief comments from the prisoner. Ruppert mentioned he'd like to have the *Wall Street Journal* delivered to his prison cell "to keep up with things." He speculated about his chances of getting to work in a prison office.

"I can type," he said.

He asked if there was a prison library where he could read. He also expressed appreciation for his aunt.

"Aunt Ruby Lee is a wonderful person, isn't she?" Ruppert asked the others in the car.

He ignored the stares of people in adjacent vehicles when they stopped at red lights. In fact, he shared, the thing that bothered him most about his trial was "crossing the street between the jail and court-house for courtroom appearances."

"The people were always there, staring at me, like I was someone infamous," Ruppert said.

He had no complaints about his treatment at the Butler County Jail. Carpenter called him a model prisoner whose quiet demeanor remained unchanged, even after his conviction and sentencing.

When the car finally stopped at the gate of the facility after a two-hour drive, Ruppert exited the vehicle and shook hands (as best as he could while handcuffed) with Perry and Carpenter. Then LoBuono walked through the gate with him. Tears appeared to form in Ruppert's eyes "as the prison gates clanged shut," Perry wrote.

The officers in the reception area greeted him by name. After he disappeared inside those walls, Ruppert never spoke to any reporter about his crime and ignored all requests for interviews.

Doug Johnson, who worked for the Butler County Sheriff's Office, transported Ruppert to a hearing several years later. He picked him up from the corrections facility in Lima, Ohio, and drove him to Hamilton. True to his reputation, Ruppert remained eerily quiet during their contact.

"He didn't say a word," Johnson recalled. "Didn't say a word. Didn't say anything."

That is, until after the day's events, when the mass murderer stepped back inside the safety of the corrections facility at Lima.

"Once we got inside the prison walls, he just opened up," Johnson said.

As they walked down a long hallway where Ruppert was housed, he pointed out the pharmacy where he got his medication, and the gymnasium where he played basketball. Johnson got a chilly feeling from his encounter with Ruppert.

"He was a quiet individual, but I felt he was an individual who could be triggered to do something horrible," Johnson added. "He was just kind of a little quiet guy, but down inside there was something else. What that was, I don't know."

While some remained haunted their entire lives by the Ruppert case and tried to forget it, others considered it an obsession.

"Not many 11-year-olds go to a murder trial," said John "JT" Thomas, who grew up across the street from the Holcomb family. "I think I went every day."

JT showed up daily with his camera and photographed Ruppert being transferred from the jail to the courthouse and vice versa. On most days, he was able to gain admittance to the courtroom and listen to the testimony. His fascination continued into his high school years and beyond, when he and his peers participated in an annual ritual of sorts.

"For years, everybody went to that house," JT said of 635 Minor Avenue. "We'd go to St. Ann's festival and then go by the Ruppert house."

Indeed, anyone who grew up in Hamilton, Ohio in the 1970s drove past that house at least once in their lives. Most cruised by it on multiple occasions. JT, however, always wanted to go inside the Ruppert house. He got his chance in 2007 or 2008, when a fellow real-estate agent landed the listing.

"It was like an out of body experience," he said. "I thought I saw somebody. It creeped me out."

He was struck by how small the house was and wondered how 11 people could even fit inside. He looked up the stairway off the kitchen, where Ruppert walked down with his weapons loaded. JT couldn't bring himself to go upstairs, but he did go down to the basement to see if the blood stains remained on the underside of the first-floor floor boards. He didn't see any.

After the showing, JT used a knife to unseal a window that had been painted shut. In the process, he accidentally sliced his finger and blood spurted from the wound.

"Now I've got my blood in the Ruppert house," he said. "You can't make this stuff up."

Chapter 41

Ruppert remained in the Chillicothe Correctional Institute for less than a month.

"It was a frightening environment for him," Frank Gray, superintendent of the facility, told the media.

Gray described Ruppert as "passive and rather fearful" during his stay.

The inmate was moved to Lima State Hospital for psychiatric treatment on August 20, 1975, after a prison psychiatrist found him to be delusional and depressed.

The appeals process dragged on for four years while Ruppert remained at the psychiatric facility. He participated in group therapy, woodworking, painting, and model building.

On April 23, 1976, all the items in what came to be known as "The Ruppert House" were sold off at a public auction, raising $2,307 amid a circus-like atmosphere. That same year, a family with two children moved into the home, after the rent had been reduced to $150 a month.

"Our friends think we're crazy," Pamela Callahan told reporter Ace Elliott after she, her husband and their two children took up occupancy there. "But we don't believe in ghosts. Anyone who did couldn't live here."

On August 3, 1977, Ohio's 1st District Court of Appeals reversed Ruppert's conviction, finding his waiver of a jury trial was not knowingly made.

In a 22-page opinion, the court found that Ruppert based his decision on misinformation that a conviction by a three-judge panel required unanimous consent from all three judges. A year later, the US Supreme Court let the decision stand and ordered a new trial for Ruppert. By that time, the death penalty had been ruled unconstitutional in Ohio and was off the table.

The town of Findlay, Ohio was the site of Ruppert's second trial. The change of venue was granted because the extensive publicity surrounding the case rendered it impossible for Ruppert to receive a fair trial in his hometown. Findlay, in Hancock County, was 140 miles away from Hamilton. Seven years had passed since the first trial.

Unlike the first trial, a jury heard the case. Holcomb again acted as lead prosecutor, assisted this time by Jim Irwin (Leonard Ruppert's former neighbor and good friend), who was appointed special assistant prosecutor for that single case. Dan Eichel—who watched every second of the first trial when he was a 23-year-old law student and summer intern in the prosecutor's office—took on the role of third-chair assistant prosecutor.

Bressler and Holbrook again defended the accused, along with attorney Tim Evans.

The six-week trial began June 14, 1982, with Visiting Judge A. Ross Siverling of Ashland County presiding. Unlike the clean-shaven defendant in the first trial, Ruppert sported a dark beard that covered his cleft chin for the second proceeding.

During the second trial, the prosecution put forth the theory that Ruppert timed the shootings to the extended pealing of the Angelus bell at St. Ann Church, a block away from Charity's house. The tolling at 6 p.m. (the estimated time of the shootings) muffled the 44 gunshots, explaining why neighbors heard nothing amiss, Holcomb argued.

Another difference in the second trial was the absence of Wanda Bishop, Ruppert's "girlfriend" from The 19th Hole.

"I think rather than being unable to find her, John chose not to call her at the second trial because she did not make such a great presentation in the 1975 trial," Eichel said. "While she had been a complete surprise to defense counsel in 1975, because they did not ask for discovery in order to keep their psychiatric and psychological insanity witnesses mostly a secret from John, Holbrock and Bressler knew who she was in 1982. They knew what she was going to say, so their cross-ex was sure to be even more blistering."

Also, the appeals court characterized Wanda as "minimally corroborated and largely contradicted" as a witness, Eichel added.

Instead of Wanda, Holcomb put on another surprise witness from The 19th Hole. John Morgan, a barber, testified that he and Ruppert conversed about the insanity defense while they were at the tavern together, roughly a month before the murders. During that conversation, Ruppert agreed with him that the insanity plea was a good way to beat a criminal charge, according to Morgan.

"A person with a history of mental illness could do almost anything—even kill somebody—and not get sent to prison or electrocuted for it," Morgan said he told a receptive Ruppert.

Morgan admitted that he found Ruppert "a little odd" and "a little old-fashioned" with his conservative attire, neat appearance and scholarly manner of speaking, but considered him of sound mind. In fact, his nickname for Ruppert was "The Psychologist."

"He tried to analyze people," Morgan said.

Others at the bar called Ruppert "The Professor," and one waitress referred to him as "Jimbo."

Once again, Ruppert did not take the stand. The jury deliberated ten and a half hours before delivering a new verdict. It found Ruppert guilty of two counts of aggravated murder in the deaths of his mother, Charity, and his brother, Leonard. The jury then found him not guilty by reason of insanity in the deaths of his sister-in-law, Alma, and her eight children.

"I think this is a footnote to the John Hinckley trial," Holcomb told a reporter after the second verdict.

The verdict indeed may have reflected the John W. Hinckley Jr. case, which dominated the news that summer. Hinckley—who attempted to assassinate President Ronald Reagan outside a Washington, DC, hotel in a misguided attempt to impress actress Jodie Foster—was found not guilty by reason of insanity on June 21, 1982. Hinckley's lawyers argued that their client suffered from narcissistic personality disorder and was re-enacting events in the 1975 movie *Taxi Driver*, which starred Foster and Robert DeNiro.

Edna Allgeier, Alma Ruppert's mother, criticized the jury's verdict and believed Ruppert deserved the electric chair. Ercel Eaton, a

longtime *Journal-News* reporter and author, described the long-suf-
fering Allgeier as a "small, wiry woman whose pain seems to be
woven into her being."

"I think sometimes I'd like to string him up on a cross like Christ,
and cut a little piece off at a time," Allgeier told *The Cincinnati Enquirer.*
"I'd want him to bleed slowly. But if you put that in the paper, people
will wonder what kind of a Catholic I am."

Allgeier held Ruppert responsible for 13 deaths—not only the
11 family members he killed on Easter Sunday 1975, but also for her
husband's suicide exactly three years to the day after the murders. She
also blamed him for the passing of juror Harold Warner, who collapsed
and died of a heart attack in the middle of the second trial.

For his crimes, Ruppert was sentenced to two consecutive life terms
in the Southern Ohio Correctional Facility. After his second trial, the
imprisoned Ruppert apparently remained obsessed with money. On
August 1, 1982, Ruppert wrote to attorney Holbrock:

> Dear Hugh,
>
> I don't have $5,000 to pay for the appeal and even if I could
> afford the appeal and I got a new trial I wouldn't be able to pay for
> the new trial so I guess the appeal is out of the question. I wish I
> had the money, I'd sure go for the appeal but I don't have it.
>
> I hope you'll continue to work hard to get me back into a mental
> hospital. That's my only hope. I could continue to draw Social
> Security checks there.
>
> Yours Truly,
> Jim Ruppert
>
> Hugh, there's no way I can call you.
>
> Hugh, if I would get a new trial I wouldn't want anybody else
> but you and Joe to try it, but as I said I wouldn't have the money
> to pay for the new trial so it's out of the question.
>
> Hope to hear from you soon.
>
> Yours Truly,
> Jim Ruppert

Hugh, I thought of a way I might raise some money.

About a year after my first trial Lucille Tabler brought an author to me; he wanted to write a book about the story of my life. He said he would gross about $70,000 and he said he would split it in half with me. While I was still in Lima I called Lucille and asked her to get in touch with him and see if he still wants to write the book. I haven't heard from her yet. I'll have to write her and see what he said. Maybe he will give me a cash advance. I'll let you know as soon as I hear from her.

Yours Truly,

Jim

Ruppert remained incarcerated until his death in a prison hospital ward on June 4, 2022. He was 88, and, unlike his 11 victims, died of natural causes. His body is buried at the Chillicothe Correctional Institute Prison Cemetery. The house at 635 Minor Avenue still stands, occupied by residents, its exterior eerily unchanged from that fateful Easter Sunday 1975.